VARIED TYPES

MORE WILDSIDE CLASSICS

Please see www.wildsidepress.com for a complete list!

VARIED TYPES

G.K. CHESTERTON

WILDSIDE PRESS

VARIED TYPES

This edition published 2005 by Wildside Press, LLC.
www.wildsidepress.com

These papers, with certain alterations and additions, are reprinted with the kind permission of the Editors of *The Daily News* and *The Speaker*.

G. K. C.
Kensington.

CONTENTS

CHARLOTTE BRONTË

Objection is often raised against realistic biography because it reveals so much that is important and even sacred about a man's life. The real objection to it will rather be found in the fact that it reveals about a man the precise points which are unimportant. It reveals and asserts and insists on exactly those things in a man's life of which the man himself is wholly unconscious; his exact class in society, the circumstances of his ancestry, the place of his present location. These are things which do not, properly speaking, ever arise before the human vision. They do not occur to a man's mind; it may be said, with almost equal truth, that they do not occur in a man's life. A man no more thinks about himself as the inhabitant of the third house in a row of Brixton villas than he thinks about himself as a strange animal with two legs. What a man's name was, what his income was, whom he married, where he lived, these are not sanctities; they are irrelevancies.

A very strong case of this is the case of the Brontës. The Brontë is in the position of the mad lady in a country village; her eccentricities form an endless source of innocent conversation to that exceedingly mild and bucolic circle, the literary world. The truly glorious gossips of literature, like Mr. Augustine Birrell and Mr. Andrew Lang, never tire of collecting all the glimpses and anecdotes and sermons and side-lights and sticks and straws which will go to make a Brontë museum. They are the most personally discussed of all Victorian authors, and the limelight of biography has left few darkened corners in the dark old Yorkshire house. And yet the whole of this biographical investigation, though natural and picturesque, is not wholly suitable to the Brontës. For the Brontë genius was above all things deputed to assert the supreme unimportance of externals. Up to that point truth had always been conceived as existing more or less in the novel of manners. Charlotte Brontë electrified the world by showing that an infinitely older and more elemental truth could be conveyed by a novel in which no person, good or bad, had any manners at all. Her work represents the first great assertion that the humdrum life of modern civilisation is a disguise as tawdry and deceptive as the costume of a *bal masqué*. She showed that abysses may exist inside a governess and eternities inside a manufacturer; her heroine is the commonplace spinster, with the dress of merino and the soul of flame. It is significant to notice that Charlotte Brontë, following consciously or unconsciously the great trend of her genius, was the first to take away from the heroine not only the artificial gold and diamonds of wealth and fashion, but even the natural gold and diamonds of physical beauty and grace. Instinctively she felt that the whole of the exterior must be made ugly that the whole of the interior might be made sublime. She chose the ugliest of women in the ugliest of centuries, and revealed within them all the hells and heavens of Dante.

It may, therefore, I think, be legitimately said that the externals of the Brontës' life, though singularly picturesque in themselves, matter less than the externals of almost any other writers. It is interesting to know whether Jane Austen had any knowledge of the lives of the officers and women of fashion whom she introduced into her masterpieces. It is interesting to know whether Dickens had ever seen a shipwreck or been inside a workhouse. For in these authors much of the conviction is conveyed, not always by adherence to facts, but always by grasp of them. But the whole aim and purport and meaning of the work of the Brontës is that the most futile thing in the whole universe is fact. Such a story as "Jane Eyre" is in itself so monstrous a fable that it ought to be excluded from a book of fairy tales. The characters do not do what they ought to do, nor what they would do, nor it might be said, such is the insanity of the atmosphere, not even what they intend to do. The conduct of Rochester is so primevally and superhumanly caddish that Bret Harte in his admirable travesty scarcely exaggerated it. "Then, resuming his usual manner, he threw his boots at my head and withdrew," does perhaps reach to something resembling caricature. The scene in which Rochester dresses up as an old gipsy has something in it which is really not to be found in any other branch of art, except in the end of the pantomime, where the Emperor turns into a pantaloon. Yet, despite this vast nightmare of illusion and morbidity and ignorance of the world, "Jane Eyre" is perhaps the truest book that was ever written. Its essential truth to life sometimes makes one catch one's breath. For it is not true to manners, which are constantly false, or to facts, which are almost always false; it is true to the only existing thing which is true, emotion, the irreducible minimum, the indestructible germ. It would not matter a single straw if a Brontë story were a hundred times more moonstruck and improbable than "Jane Eyre," or a hundred times more moonstruck and improbable than "Wuthering Heights." It would not matter if George Read stood on his head, and Mrs. Read rode on a dragon, if Fairfax Rochester had four eyes and St. John Rivers three legs, the story would still remain the truest story in the world. The typical Brontë character is, indeed, a kind of monster. Everything in him except the essential is dislocated. His hands are on his legs and his feet on his arms, his nose is above his eyes, but his heart is in the right place.

The great and abiding truth for which the Brontë cycle of fiction stands is a certain most important truth about the enduring spirit of youth, the truth of the near kinship between terror and joy. The Brontë heroine, dingily dressed, badly educated, hampered by a humiliating inexperience, a kind of ugly innocence, is yet, by the very fact of her solitude and her gaucherie, full of the greatest delight that is possible to a human being, the delight of expectation, the delight of an ardent and flamboyant ignorance. She serves to show how futile it is of humanity to suppose that pleasure can be attained chiefly by putting on evening dress every evening, and having a box at the theatre every first night. It is not the man of pleasure who has pleasure; it is not the man of the world who appreciates the world. The man who has learnt to do all conventional things perfectly has at the same time learnt to do them prosaically. It is the awkward man, whose evening dress does not fit him, whose gloves will not go on, whose compliments will not come off, who is really full of the ancient ecstasies of youth. He is frightened enough of society actually to enjoy his triumphs. He has that element of fear which is one of the eternal ingredients of joy. This spirit is the central spirit of the Brontë novel. It is the epic of the exhilaration of the shy man. As such it is of incalculable value in our time, of which the curse is that it does not take joy reverently because it does not take it fearfully. The shabby and inconspicuous governess of Charlotte Brontë, with the small outlook and the small creed, had more commerce with the awful and elemental forces which drive the world than a legion of lawless minor poets. She approached the universe with real simplicity, and, consequently, with real fear and delight. She was, so to speak, shy before the multitude of the stars, and in this she had possessed herself of the only force which can prevent enjoyment being as black and barren as routine. The faculty of being shy is the first and the most delicate of the powers of enjoyment. The fear of the Lord is the beginning of pleasure.

Upon the whole, therefore, I think it may justifiably be said that the dark wild youth of the Brontës in their dark wild Yorkshire home has been somewhat exaggerated as a necessary factor in their work and their conception. The emotions with which they dealt were universal emotions, emotions of the morning of existence, the springtide joy and the springtide terror. Every one of us as a boy or girl has had some midnight dream of nameless obstacle and unutterable menace, in which there was, under whatever imbecile forms, all the deadly stress and panic of "Wuthering Heights." Every one of us has had a day-dream of our own potential destiny not one atom more reasonable than "Jane Eyre." And the truth which the Brontës came to tell us is the truth that many waters cannot quench love, and that suburban respectability cannot touch or damp a secret enthusiasm. Clapham, like every other earthly city, is built upon a volcano. Thousands of people go to and fro in the wilderness of bricks and mortar, earning mean wages, professing a mean religion, wearing a mean attire, thousands of women who have never found any expression for their exaltation or their tragedy but to go on working harder and yet harder at dull and automatic employments, at scolding children or stitching shirts. But out of all these silent ones one suddenly became articulate, and spoke a resonant testimony, and her name was Charlotte Brontë. Spreading around us upon every side today like a huge and radiating geometrical figure are the endless branches of the great city. There are times when we are almost stricken crazy, as well we may be, by the multiplicity of those appalling perspectives, the frantic arithmetic of that unthinkable population. But this thought of ours is in truth nothing but a fancy. There are no chains of houses; there are no crowds of men. The colossal diagram of streets and houses is an illusion, the opium dream of a speculative builder. Each of these men is supremely solitary and supremely important to himself. Each of these houses stands in the centre of the world. There is no single house of all those millions which has not seemed to someone at some time the heart of all things and the end of travel.

WILLIAM MORRIS
AND HIS SCHOOL

It is proper enough that the unveiling of the bust of William Morris should approximate to a public festival, for while there have been many men of genius in the Victorian era more despotic than he, there have been none so representative. He represents not only that rapacious hunger for beauty which has now for the first time become a serious problem in the healthy life of humanity, but he represents also that honourable instinct for finding beauty in common necessities of workmanship which gives it a stronger and more bony structure. The time has passed when William Morris was conceived to be irrelevant to be described as a designer of wall-papers. If Morris had been a hatter instead of a decorator, we should have become gradually and painfully conscious of an improvement in our hats. If he had been a tailor, we should have suddenly found our frock-coats trailing on the ground with the grandeur of mediæval raiment. If he had been a shoemaker, we should have found, with no little consternation, our shoes gradually approximating to the antique sandal. As a hairdresser, he would have invented some massing of the hair worthy to be the crown of Venus; as an ironmonger, his nails would have had some noble pattern, fit to be the nails of the Cross.

The limitations of William Morris, whatever they were, were not the limitations of common decoration. It is true that all his work, even his literary work, was in some sense decorative, had in some degree the qualities of a splendid wall-paper. His characters, his stories, his religious and political views, had, in the most emphatic sense, length and breadth without thickness. He seemed really to believe that men could enjoy a perfectly flat felicity. He made no account of the unexplored and explosive possibilities of human nature, of the unnameable terrors, and the yet more unnameable hopes. So long as a man was graceful in every circumstance, so long as he had the inspiring consciousness that the chestnut colour of his hair was relieved against the blue forest a mile behind, he would be serenely happy. So he would be, no doubt, if he were really fitted for a decorative existence; if he were a piece of exquisitely coloured card-board.

But although Morris took little account of the terrible solidity of human nature—took little account, so to speak, of human figures in the round, it is altogether unfair to represent him as a mere æsthete. He perceived a great public necessity and fulfilled it heroically. The difficulty with which he grappled was one so immense that we shall have to be separated from it by many centuries before we can really judge of it. It was the problem of the elaborate and deliberate ugliness of the most self-conscious of centuries. Morris at least saw the absurdity of the thing. He felt it was monstrous that the modern man, who was pre-eminently capable of realising the strangest and most contradictory beauties, who could feel at once the fiery aureole of the ascetic and the colossal calm of the Hellenic god, should himself, by a farcical bathos, be buried in a black coat, and hidden under a chimney-pot hat. He could not see why the harmless man who desired to be an artist in raiment should be condemned to be, at best, a black and white artist. It is indeed difficult to account for the clinging curse of ugliness which blights everything brought forth by the most prosperous of centuries. In all created nature there is not, perhaps, anything so completely ugly as a pillar-box. Its shape is the most unmeaning of shapes, its height and thickness just neutralising each other; its colour is the most repulsive of colours—a fat and soulless red, a red without a touch of blood or fire, like the scarlet of dead men's sins. Yet there is no reason whatever why such hideousness should possess an object full of civic dignity, the treasure-house of a thousand secrets, the fortress of a thousand souls. If the old Greeks had had such an institution, we may be sure that it would have been surmounted by the severe, but graceful, figure of the god of letter-writing. If the mediæval Christians has possessed it, it would have had a niche filled with the golden aureole of St. Rowland of the Postage Stamps. As it is, there it stands at all our street-corners, disguising one of the most beautiful of ideas under one of the most preposterous of forms. It is useless to deny that the miracles of science have not been such an incentive to art and imagination as were the miracles of religion. If men in the twelfth century had been told that the lightning had been driven for leagues underground, and had dragged at its destroying tail loads of laughing human beings, and if they had then been told that the people alluded to this pulverising portent chirpily as "The Twopenny Tube," they would have called down the fire of Heaven on us as a race of halfwitted atheists. Probably they would have been quite right.

This clear and fine perception of what may be called the anæsthetic element in the Victorian era was, undoubtedly, the work of a great reformer: it requires a fine effort of the imagination to see an evil that surrounds us on every side. The manner in which Morris carried out his crusade may, considering the circumstances, be called triumphant. Our carpets began to bloom under our feet like the meadows in spring, and our hitherto prosaic stools and sofas seemed growing legs and arms at their own wild will. An element of freedom and rugged dignity came in with plain and strong ornaments of copper and iron. So delicate and universal has been the revolution in domestic art that almost every family in England has had its taste cunningly and treacherously improved, and if we look back at the early Victorian drawing-rooms it is only to realise the strange but essential truth that art, or human decoration, has, nine times out of ten in history, made things uglier than they were before, from the "coiffure" of a Papuan savage to the wall-paper of a British merchant in 1830.

But great and beneficent as was the æsthetic revolution of Morris, there was a very definite limit to it. It did not lie only in the fact that his revolution was in truth a reaction, though this was a partial explanation of his partial failure. When he was denouncing the dresses of modern ladies, "upholstered like armchairs instead of being draped like women," as he forcibly expressed it, he would hold up for practical imitation the costumes and handicrafts of the Middle Ages. Further than this retrogressive and imitative movement he never seemed to go. Now, the men of the time of Chaucer had many evil qualities, but there was at least one exhibition of moral weakness they did not give. They would have laughed at the idea of dressing themselves in the manner of the bowmen at the battle of Senlac, or painting themselves an æsthetic blue, after the custom of the ancient Britons. They would not have called that a movement at all. Whatever was beautiful in their dress or manners sprang honestly and naturally out of the life they led and preferred to lead. And it may surely be maintained that any real advance in the beauty of modern dress must spring honestly and naturally out of the life we lead and prefer to lead. We are not altogether without hints and hopes of such a change, in the growing orthodoxy of rough and athletic costumes. But if this cannot be, it will be no substitute or satisfaction to turn life into an interminable historical fancy-dress ball.

But the limitation of Morris's work lay deeper than this. We may best suggest it by a method after his own heart. Of all the various works he performed, none, perhaps, was so splendidly and solidly valuable as his great protest for the fables and superstitions of mankind. He has the supreme credit of showing that the fairy tales contain the deepest truth of the earth, the real record of men's feeling for things. Trifling details may be inaccurate, Jack may not have climbed up so tall a beanstalk, or killed so tall a giant; but it is not such things that make a story false; it is a far different class of things that makes every modern book of history as false as the father of lies; ingenuity, self-consciousness, hypocritical impartiality. It appears to us that of all the fairy-tales none contains so vital a moral truth as the old story, existing in many forms, of Beauty and the Beast. There is written, with all the authority of a human scripture, the eternal and essential truth that until we love a thing in all its ugliness we cannot make it beautiful. This was the weak point in William Morris as a reformer: that he sought to reform modern life, and that he hated modern life instead of loving it. Modern London is indeed a beast, big enough and black enough to be the beast in Apocalypse, blazing with a million eyes, and roaring with a million voices. But unless the poet can love this fabulous monster as he is, can feel with some generous excitement his massive and mysterious *joie-de-vivre*, the vast scale of his iron anatomy and the beating of his thunderous heart, he cannot and will not change the beast into the fairy prince. Morris's disadvantage was that he was not honestly a child of the nineteenth century: he could not understand its fascination, and consequently he could not really develop it. An abiding testimony to his tremendous personal influence in the æsthetic world is the vitality and recurrence of the Arts and Crafts Exhibitions, which are steeped in his personality like a chapel in that of a saint. If we look round at the exhibits in one of these æsthetic shows, we shall be struck by the large mass of modern objects that the decorative school leaves untouched. There is a noble instinct for giving the right touch of beauty to common and necessary things, but the things that are so touched are the ancient things, the things that always to some extent commended themselves to the lover of beauty. There are beautiful gates, beautiful fountains, beautiful cups, beautiful chairs, beautiful reading-desks. But there are no modern things made beautiful. There are no beautiful lamp-posts, beautiful letter-boxes, beautiful engines, beautiful bicycles. The spirit of William Morris has not seized hold of the century and made its humblest necessities beautiful. And this was because, with all his healthiness and energy, he had not the supreme courage to face the ugliness of things; Beauty shrank from the Beast and the fairy-tale had a different ending.

But herein, indeed, lay Morris's deepest claim to the name of a great reformer: that he left his work incomplete. There is, perhaps, no better proof that a man is a mere meteor, merely barren and brilliant, than that his work is done perfectly. A man like Morris draws attention to needs he cannot supply. In after-years we may have perhaps a newer and more daring Arts and Crafts Exhibition. In it we shall not decorate the armour of the twelfth century, but the machinery of the twentieth. A lamp-post shall be wrought nobly in twisted iron, fit to hold the sanctity of fire. A pillar-box shall be carved with figures emblematical of the secrets of comradeship and the silence and honour of the State. Railway signals, of all earthly things the most poetical, the coloured stars of life and death, shall be lamps of green and crimson worthy of their terrible and faithful service. But if ever this gradual and genuine movement of our time towards beauty—not backwards, but forwards—does truly come about, Morris will be the first prophet of it. Poet of the childhood of nations, craftsman in the new honesties of art, prophet of a merrier and wiser life, his full-blooded enthusiasm will be remembered when human life has once more assumed flamboyant colours and proved that this painful greenish grey of the æsthetic twilight in which we now live is, in spite of all the pessimists, not of the greyness of death, but the greyness of dawn.

THE OPTIMISM
OF BYRON

Everything is against our appreciating the spirit and the age of Byron. The age that has just passed from us is always like a dream when we wake in the morning, a thing incredible and centuries away. And the world of Byron seems a sad and faded world, a weird and inhuman world, where men were romantic in whiskers, ladies lived, apparently, in bowers, and the very word has the sound of a piece of stage scenery. Roses and nightingales recur in their poetry with the monotonous elegance of a wall-paper pattern. The whole is like a revel of dead men, a revel with splendid vesture and halfwitted faces.

But the more shrewdly and earnestly we study the histories of men, the less ready shall we be to make use of the word "artificial." Nothing in the world has ever been artificial. Many customs, many dresses, many works of art are branded with artificiality because they exhibit vanity and self-consciousness: as if vanity were not a deep and elemental thing, like love and hate and the fear of death. Vanity may be found in darkling deserts, in the hermit and in the wild beasts that crawl around him. It may be good or evil, but assuredly it is not artificial: vanity is a voice out of the abyss.

The remarkable fact is, however, and it bears strongly on the present position of Byron, that when a thing is unfamiliar to us, when it is remote and the product of some other age or spirit, we think it not savage or terrible, but merely artificial. There are many instances of this: a fair one is the case of tropical plants and birds. When we see some of the monstrous and flamboyant blossoms that enrich the equatorial woods, we do not feel that they are conflagrations of nature; silent explosions of her frightful energy. We simply find it hard to believe that they are not wax flowers grown under a glass case. When we see some of the tropic birds, with their tiny bodies attached to gigantic beaks, we do not feel that they are freaks of the fierce humour of Creation. We almost believe that they are toys out of a child's play-box, artificially carved and artificially coloured. So it is with the great convulsion of Nature which was known as Byronism. The volcano is not an extinct volcano now; it is the dead stick of a rocket. It is the remains not of a natural but of an artificial fire.

But Byron and Byronism were something immeasurably greater than anything that is represented by such a view as this: their real value and meaning are indeed little understood. The first of the mistakes about Byron lies in the fact that he is treated as a pessimist. True, he treated himself as such, but a critic can hardly have even a slight knowledge of Byron without knowing that he had the smallest amount of knowledge of himself that ever fell to the lot of an intelligent man. The real character of what is known as Byron's pessimism is better worth study than any real pessimism could ever be.

It is the standing peculiarity of this curious world of ours that almost everything in it has been extolled enthusiastically and invariably extolled to the disadvantage of everything else.

One after another almost every one of the phenomena of the universe has been declared to be alone capable of making life worth living. Books, love, business, religion, alcohol, abstract truth, private emotion, money, simplicity, mysticism, hard work, a life close to nature, a life close to Belgrave Square are every one of them passionately maintained by somebody to be so good that they redeem the evil of an otherwise indefensible world. Thus, while the world is almost always condemned in summary, it is always justified, and indeed extolled, in detail after detail.

Existence has been praised and absolved by a chorus of pessimists. The work of giving thanks to Heaven is, as it were, divided ingeniously among them. Schopenhauer is told off as a kind of librarian in the House of God, to sing the praises of the austere pleasures of the mind. Carlyle, as steward, undertakes the working department and eulogises a life of labour in the fields. Omar Khayyam is established in the cellar, and swears that it is the only room in the house. Even the blackest of pessimistic artists enjoys his art. At the precise moment that he has written some shameless and terrible indictment of Creation, his one pang of joy in the achievement joins the universal chorus of gratitude, with the scent of the wild flower and the song of the bird.

Now Byron had a sensational popularity, and that popularity

was, as far as words and explanations go, founded upon his pessimism. He was adored by an overwhelming majority, almost every individual of which despised the majority of mankind. But when we come to regard the matter a little more deeply we tend in some degree to cease to believe in this popularity of the pessimist. The popularity of pure and unadulterated pessimism is an oddity; it is almost a contradiction in terms. Men would no more receive the news of the failure of existence or of the harmonious hostility of the stars with ardour or popular rejoicing than they would light bonfires for the arrival of cholera or dance a breakdown when they were condemned to be hanged. When the pessimist is popular it must always be not because he shows all things to be bad, but because he shows some things to be good.

Men can only join in a chorus of praise, even if it is the praise of denunciation. The man who is popular must be optimistic about something, even if he is only optimistic about pessimism. And this was emphatically the case with Byron and the Byronists. Their real popularity was founded not upon the fact that they blamed everything, but upon the fact that they praised something. They heaped curses upon man, but they used man merely as a foil. The things they wished to praise by comparison were the energies of Nature. Man was to them what talk and fashion were to Carlyle, what philosophical and religious quarrels were to Omar, what the whole race after practical happiness was to Schopenhauer, the thing which must be censured in order that somebody else may be exalted. It was merely a recognition of the fact that one cannot write in white chalk except on a black-board.

Surely it is ridiculous to maintain seriously that Byron's love of the desolate and inhuman in nature was the mark of vital scepticism and depression. When a young man can elect deliberately to walk alone in winter by the side of the shattering sea, when he takes pleasure in storms and stricken peaks, and the lawless melancholy of the older earth, we may deduce with the certainty of logic that he is very young and very happy. There is a certain darkness which we see in wine when seen in shadow; we see it again in the night that has just buried a gorgeous sunset. The wine seems black, and yet at the same time powerfully and almost impossibly red; the sky seems black, and yet at the same time to be only too dense a blend of purple and green. Such was the darkness which lay around the Byronic school. Darkness with them was only too dense a purple. They would prefer the sullen hostility of the earth because amid all the cold and darkness their own hearts were flaming like their own firesides.

Matters are very different with the more modern school of doubt and lamentation. The last movement of pessimism is perhaps expressed in Mr. Aubrey Beardsley's allegorical designs. Here we have to deal with a pessimism which tends naturally not towards the oldest elements of the cosmos, but towards the last and most fantastic fripperies of artificial life. Byronism tended towards the desert; the new pessimism towards the restaurant. Byronism was a revolt against artificiality; the new pessimism is a revolt in its favour.

The Byronic young man had an affectation of sincerity; the decadent, going a step deeper into the avenues of the unreal, has positively an affectation of affectation. And it is by their fopperies and their frivolities that we know that their sinister philosophy is sincere; in their lights and garlands and ribbons we read their indwelling despair. It was so, indeed, with Byron himself; his really bitter moments were his frivolous moments. He went on year after year calling down fire upon mankind, summoning the deluge and the destructive sea and all the ultimate energies of nature to sweep away the cities of the spawn of man. But through all this his subconscious mind was not that of a despairer; on the contrary, there is something of a kind of lawless faith in thus parleying with such immense and immemorial brutalities. It was not until the time in which he wrote "Don Juan" that he really lost this inward warmth and geniality, and a sudden shout of hilarious laughter announced to the world that Lord Byron had really become a pessimist.

One of the best tests in the world of what a poet really means is his metre. He may be a hypocrite in his metaphysics, but he cannot be a hypocrite in his prosody. And all the time that Byron's language is of horror and emptiness, his metre is a bounding *pas de quatre*. He may arraign existence on the most deadly charges, he may condemn it with the most desolating verdict, but he cannot alter the fact that on some walk in a spring morning when all the limbs are swinging and all the blood alive in the body, the lips may be caught repeating:

"Oh, there's not a joy the world can give like that it takes away,

When the glow of early youth declines in beauty's dull decay;
'Tis not upon the cheek of youth the blush that fades so fast,
But the tender bloom of heart is gone ere youth itself be past."

That automatic recitation is the answer to the whole pessimism of Byron.

The truth is that Byron was one of a class who may be called the unconscious optimists, who are very often, indeed, the most uncompromising conscious pessimists, because the exuberance of their nature demands for an adversary a dragon as big as the world. But the whole of his essential and unconscious being was spirited and confident, and that unconscious being, long disguised and buried under emotional artifices, suddenly sprang into prominence in the face of a cold, hard, political necessity. In Greece he heard the cry of reality, and at the time that he was dying, he began to live. He heard suddenly the call of that buried and subconscious happiness which is in all of us, and which may emerge suddenly at the sight of the grass of a meadow or the spears of the enemy.

POPE AND
THE ART OF SATIRE

The general critical theory common in this and the last century is that it was very easy for the imitators of Pope to write English poetry. The classical couplet was a thing that anyone could do. So far as that goes, one may justifiably answer by asking anyone to try. It may be easier really to have wit, than really, in the boldest and most enduring sense, to have imagination. But it is immeasurably easier to pretend to have imagination than to pretend to have wit. A man may indulge in a sham rhapsody, because it may be the triumph of a rhapsody to be unintelligible. But a man cannot indulge in a sham joke, because it is the ruin of a joke to be unintelligible. A man may pretend to be a poet: he can no more pretend to be a wit than he can pretend to bring rabbits out of a hat without having learnt to be a conjuror. Therefore, it may be submitted, there was a certain discipline in the old antithetical couplet of Pope and his followers. If it did not permit of the great liberty of wisdom used by the minority of great geniuses, neither did it permit of the great liberty of folly which is used by the majority of small writers. A prophet could not be a poet in those days, perhaps, but at least a fool could not be a poet. If we take, for the sake of example, such a line as Pope's:

"Damn with faint praise, assent with civil leer,"

the test is comparatively simple. A great poet would not have written such a line, perhaps. But a minor poet could not.

Supposing that a lyric poet of the new school really had to deal with such an idea as that expressed in Pope's line about Man:

"A being darkly wise and rudely great,"

Is it really so certain that he would go deeper into the matter than that old antithetical jingle goes? I venture to doubt whether he would really be any wiser or weirder or more imaginative or more profound. The one thing that he would really be, would be longer. Instead of writing,

"A being darkly wise and rudely great,"

the contemporary poet, in his elaborately ornamented book of verses, would produce something like the following:

"A creature
Of feature
More dark, more dark, more dark than skies,
Yea, darkly wise, yea, darkly wise:
Darkly wise as a formless fate.
And if he be great,
If he be great, then rudely great,
Rudely great as a plough that plies,
And darkly wise, and darkly wise."

Have we really learnt to think more broadly? Or have we only learnt to spread our thoughts thinner? I have a dark suspicion that a modern poet might manufacture an admirable lyric out of almost every line of Pope.

There is, of course, an idea in our time that the very antithesis of the typical line of Pope is a mark of artificiality. I shall have occasion more than once to point out that nothing in the world has ever been artificial. But certainly antithesis is not artificial. An element of paradox runs through the whole of existence itself. It begins in the realm of ultimate physics and metaphysics, in the two facts that we cannot imagine a space that is infinite, and that we cannot imagine a space that is finite. It runs through the inmost complications of divinity, in that we cannot conceive that Christ in the wilderness was truly pure, unless we also conceive that he desired to sin. It runs, in the same manner, through all the minor matters of morals, so that we cannot imagine courage existing except in conjunction with fear, or magnanimity existing except in conjunction with some temptation to meanness. If Pope and his followers caught this echo of natural irrationality, they were not any the more artificial. Their antitheses were fully in harmony with existence, which is itself a contradiction in terms.

Pope was really a great poet; he was the last great poet of civilisation. Immediately after the fall of him and his school come Burns and Byron, and the reaction towards the savage and the elemental. But to Pope civilisation was still an exciting experiment. Its perruques and ruffles were to him what feathers and bangles are to a South Sea Islander—the real romance of civilisation. And in all the forms of art which peculiarly belong to civilisation, he was supreme. In one especially he was supreme—the great and civilised art of satire. And in this we have fallen away utterly.

We have had a great revival in our time of the cult of violence and hostility. Mr. Henley and his young men have an infinite number of furious epithets with which to overwhelm anyone who differs from them. It is not a placid or untroubled position to be Mr. Henley's enemy, though we know that it is certainly safer than to be his friend. And yet, despite all this, these people produce no satire. Political and social satire is a lost art, like pottery and stained glass. It may be worth while to make some attempt to point out a reason for this.

It may seem a singular observation to say that we are not generous enough to write great satire. This, however, is approximately a very accurate way of describing the case. To write great satire, to attack a man so that he feels the attack and half acknowledges its justice, it is necessary to have a certain intellectual magnanimity which realises the merits of the opponent as well as his defects. This is, indeed, only another way of putting the simple truth that in order to attack an army we must know not only its weak points, but also its strong points. England in the present season and spirit fails in satire for the same simple reason that it fails in war: it despises the enemy. In matters of battle and conquest we have got firmly rooted in our minds the idea (an idea fit for the philosophers of Bedlam) that we can best trample on a people by ignoring all the particular merits which give them a chance of trampling upon us. It has become a breach of etiquette to praise the enemy; whereas, when the enemy is strong, every honest scout ought to praise the enemy. It is impossible to vanquish an army without having a full account of its strength. It is impossible to satirise a man without having a full account of his virtues. It is too much the custom in politics to describe a political opponent as utterly inhuman, as utterly careless of his country, as utterly cynical, which no man ever was since the beginning of the world. This kind of invective may often have a great superficial success: it may hit the mood of the moment; it may raise excitement and applause; it may impress millions. But there is one man among all those millions whom it does not impress, whom it hardly ever touches; that is the man against whom it is directed. The one person for whom the whole satire has been written in vain is the man whom it is the whole object of the institution of satire to reach. He knows that such a description of him is not true. He knows that he is not utterly unpatriotic, or utterly self-seeking, or utterly barbarous and revengeful. He knows that he is an ordinary man, and that he can count as many kindly memories, as many humane instincts, as many hours of decent work and responsibility as any other ordinary man. But behind all this he has his real weaknesses, the real ironies of his soul: behind all these ordinary merits lie the mean compromises, the craven silences, the sullen vanities, the secret brutalities, the unmanly visions of revenge. It is to these that satire should reach if it is to touch the man at whom it is aimed. And to reach these it must pass and salute a whole army of virtues.

If we turn to the great English satirists of the seventeenth and eighteenth centuries, for example, we find that they had this rough, but firm, grasp of the size and strength, the value and the best points of their adversary. Dryden, before hewing Ahitophel in pieces, gives a splendid and spirited account of the insane valour and inspired cunning of the

"daring pilot in extremity,"

who was more untrustworthy in calm than in storm, and

"Steered too near the rocks to boast his wit."

The whole is, so far as it goes, a sound and picturesque version of the great Shaftesbury. It would, in many ways, serve as a very sound and picturesque account of Lord Randolph Churchill. But here comes in very pointedly the difference between our modern attempts at satire and the ancient achievement of it. The opponents of Lord Randolph Churchill, both Liberal and Conservative, did not satirise him nobly and honestly, as one of those great wits to madness near allied. They represented him as a mere puppy, a silly and irreverent upstart whose impudence supplied the lack of policy and character. Churchill had grave and even gross faults, a certain coarseness, a certain hard boyish assertiveness, a certain lack of magnanimity, a certain peculiar patrician vulgarity. But he was a much larger man than satire depicted him, and therefore the satire could not and did not overwhelm him. And here we have the cause of the failure of contemporary satire, that it has no magnanimity, that is to say, no patience. It cannot endure to be told that its opponent has his strong points, just as Mr. Chamberlain could not endure to be told that the Boers had a regular army. It can be content with nothing except persuading itself that its opponent is utterly bad or utterly stupid—that is, that he is what he is not and what nobody else is. If we take any prominent politician of the day—such, for example, as Sir William Harcourt—we shall find that this is the point in which all party invective fails. The Tory satire at the expense of Sir William Harcourt is always desperately endeavouring to represent that he is inept, that he makes a fool of himself, that he is disagreeable and disgraceful and untrustworthy. The defect of all that is that we all know that it is untrue. Everyone knows that Sir William Harcourt is not inept, but is almost the ablest Parliamentarian now alive. Everyone knows that he is not disagreeable or disgraceful, but a gentleman of the old school who is on excellent social terms with his antagonists. Everyone knows that he is not untrustworthy, but a man of unimpeachable honour who is much trusted. Above all, he knows it himself, and is therefore affected by the satire exactly as any one of us would be if we were accused of being black or of keeping a shop for the receiving of stolen goods. We might be angry at the libel, but not at the satire: for a man is angry at a libel because it is false, but at a satire because it is true.

Mr. Henley and his young men are very fond of invective and satire; if they wish to know the reason of their failure in these things, they need only turn to the opening of Pope's superb attack upon Addison. The Henleyite's idea of satirising a man is to express a violent contempt for him, and by the heat of this to persuade others and himself that the man is contemptible. I remember reading a satiric attack on Mr. Gladstone by one of the young anarchic Tories, which began by asserting that Mr. Gladstone was a bad public speaker. If these people would, as I have said, go quietly and read Pope's "Atticus," they would see how a great satirist approaches a great enemy:

> *"Peace to all such! But were there one whose fires*
> *True genius kindles, and fair fame inspires,*
> *Blest with each talent, and each art to please,*
> *And born to write, converse, and live with ease.*
> *Should such a man—"*

And then follows the torrent of that terrible criticism. Pope was not such a fool as to try to make out that Addison was a fool. He knew that Addison was not a fool, and he knew that Addison knew it. But hatred, in Pope's case, had become so great and, I was almost going to say, so pure, that it illuminated all things, as love illuminates all things. He said what was really wrong with Addison; and in calm and clear and everlasting colours he painted the picture of the evil of the literary temperament:

> *"Bear, like the Turk, no brother near the throne,*
> *View him with scornful, yet with jealous eyes,*
> *And hate for arts that caused himself to rise.*
> *   *   *   *   *   **
> *Like Cato give his little Senate laws,*
> *And sit attentive to his own applause.*
> *While wits and templars every sentence raise,*
> *And wonder with a foolish face of praise."*

This is the kind of thing which really goes to the mark at which it aims. It is penetrated with sorrow and a kind of reverence, and it is addressed directly to a man. This is no mock-tournament to gain the applause of the crowd. It is a deadly duel by the lonely seashore.

In current political materialism there is everywhere the assumption that, without understanding anything of his case or his merits, we can benefit a man practically. Without understanding his case and his merits, we cannot even hurt him.

FRANCIS

Asceticism is a thing which, in its very nature, we tend in these days to misunderstand. Asceticism, in the religious sense, is the repudiation of the great mass of human joys because of the supreme joyfulness of the one joy, the religious joy. But asceticism is not in the least confined to religious asceticism: there is scientific asceticism which asserts that truth is alone satisfying: there is æsthetic asceticism which asserts that art is alone satisfying: there is amatory asceticism which asserts that love is alone satisfying. There is even epicurean asceticism, which asserts that beer and skittles are alone satisfying. Wherever the manner of praising anything involves the statement that the speaker could live with that thing alone, there lies the germ and essence of asceticism. When William Morris, for example, says that "love is enough," it is obvious that he asserts in those words that art, science, politics, ambition, money, houses, carriages, concerts, gloves, walking-sticks, door-knockers, railway-stations, cathedrals, and any other things one may choose to tabulate are unnecessary. When Omar Khayyam says:

> *"A book of verses underneath the bough,*
> *A loaf of bread, a jug of wine, and thou*
> *Beside me singing in the wilderness—*
> *O wilderness were Paradise enow."*

It is clear that he speaks fully as much ascetically as he does æsthetically. He makes a list of things and says that he wants no more. The same thing was done by a mediæval monk. Examples might, of course, be multiplied a hundred-fold. One of the most genuinely poetical of our younger poets says, as the one thing certain, that

> *"From quiet home and first beginning*
> *Out to the undiscovered ends—*
> *There's nothing worth the wear of winning*

But laughter and the love of friends."

Here we have a perfect example of the main important fact, that all true joy expresses itself in terms of asceticism.

But if, in any case, it should happen that a class or a generation lose the sense of the peculiar kind of joy which is being celebrated, they immediately begin to call the enjoyers of that joy gloomy and self-destroying. The most formidable liberal philosophers have called the monks melancholy because they denied themselves the pleasures of liberty and marriage. They might as well call the trippers on a Bank Holiday melancholy because they deny themselves, as a rule, the pleasures of silence and meditation. A simpler and stronger example is, however, to hand. If ever it should happen that the system of English athletics should vanish from the public schools and the universities, if science should supply some new and non-competitive manner of perfecting the physique, if public ethics swung round to an attitude of absolute contempt and indifference towards the feeling called sport, then it is easy to see what would happen. Future historians would simply state that in the dark days of Queen Victoria young men at Oxford and Cambridge were subjected to a horrible sort of religious torture. They were forbidden, by fantastic monastic rules, to indulge in wine or tobacco during certain arbitrarily fixed periods of time, before certain brutal fights and festivals. Bigots insisted on their rising at unearthly hours and running violently around fields for no object. Many men ruined their health in these dens of superstition, many died there. All this is perfectly true and irrefutable. Athleticism in England is an asceticism, as much as the monastic rules. Men have overstrained themselves and killed themselves through English athleticism. There is one difference and one only: we do feel the love of sport; we do not feel the love of religious offices. We see only the price in the one case and only the purchase in the other.

The only question that remains is what was the joy of the old Christian ascetics of which their asceticism was merely the purchasing price? The mere possibility of the query is an extraordinary example of the way in which we miss the main points of human history. We are looking at humanity too close, and see only the details and not the vast and dominant features. We look at the rise of Christianity, and conceive it as a rise of self-abnegation and almost of pessimism. It does not occur to us that the mere assertion that this raging and confounding universe is governed by justice and mercy is a piece of staggering optimism fit to set all men capering. The detail over which these monks went mad with joy was the universe itself; the only thing really worthy of enjoyment. The white daylight shone over all the world, the endless forests stood up in their order. The lightning awoke and the tree fell and the sea gathered into mountains and the ship went down, and all these disconnected and meaningless and terrible objects were all part of one dark and fearful conspiracy of goodness, one merciless scheme of mercy. That this scheme of Nature was not accurate or well founded is perfectly tenable, but surely it is not tenable that it was not optimistic. We insist, however, upon treating this matter tail foremost. We insist that the ascetics were pessimists because they gave up threescore years and ten for an eternity of happiness. We forget that the bare proposition of an eternity of happiness is by its very nature ten thousand times more optimistic than ten thousand pagan saturnalias.

Mr. Adderley's life of Francis of Assisi does not, of course, bring this out; nor does it fully bring out the character of Francis. It has rather the tone of a devotional book. A devotional book is an excellent thing, but we do not look in it for the portrait of a man, for the same reason that we do not look in a love-sonnet for the portrait of a woman, because men in such conditions of mind not only apply all virtues to their idol, but all virtues in equal quantities. There is no outline, because the artist cannot bear to put in a black line. This blaze of benediction, this conflict between lights, has its place in poetry, not in biography. The successful examples of it may be found, for instance, in the more idealistic odes of Spenser. The design is sometimes almost indecipherable, for the poet draws in silver upon white.

It is natural, of course, that Mr. Adderley should see Francis primarily as the founder of the Franciscan Order. We suspect this was only one, perhaps a minor one, of the things that he was; we suspect that one of the minor things that Christ did was to found Christianity. But the vast practical work of Francis is assuredly not to be ignored, for this amazingly unworldly and almost maddeningly simple-minded infant was one of the most consistently successful men that ever fought with this bitter world. It is the custom to say that the secret of such men is their profound belief in themselves, and this is true, but not all the truth. Workhouses and lunatic asylums are thronged with men who believe in themselves. Of Francis it is far truer to say that the secret of his success was his profound belief in other people, and it is the lack of this that has commonly been the curse of these obscure Napoleons. Francis always assumed that everyone must be just as anxious about their common relative, the water-rat, as he was. He planned a visit to the Emperor to draw his attention to the needs of "his little sisters the larks." He used to talk to any thieves and robbers he met about their misfortune in being unable to give rein to their desire for holiness. It was an innocent habit, and doubtless the robbers often "got round him," as the phrase goes. Quite as often, however, they discovered that he had "got round" them, and discovered the other side, the side of secret nobility.

Conceiving of St. Francis as primarily the founder of the Franciscan Order, Mr. Adderley opens his narrative with an admirable sketch of the history of Monasticism in Europe, which is certainly the best thing in the book. He distinguishes clearly and fairly between the Manichæan ideal that underlies so much of Eastern Monasticism and the ideal of self-discipline which never wholly vanished from the Christian form. But he does not throw any light on what must be for the outsider the absorbing problem of this Catholic asceticism, for the excellent reason that, not being an outsider, he does not find it a problem at all.

To most people, however, there is a fascinating inconsistency in the position of St. Francis. He expressed in loftier and bolder language than any earthly thinker the conception that laughter is as divine as tears. He called his monks the mountebanks of God. He never forgot to take pleasure in a bird as it flashed past him, or a drop of water, as it fell from his finger: he was, perhaps, the happiest of the sons of men. Yet this man undoubtedly founded his whole polity on the negation of what we think the most imperious necessities; in his three vows of poverty, chastity, and obedience, he denied to himself and those he loved most, property, love, and liberty. Why was it that the most large-hearted and poetic spirits in that age found their most congenial atmosphere in these awful renunciations? Why did he who loved where all men were blind, seek to blind himself where all men loved? Why was he a monk, and not a troubadour? These questions are far too large to be answered fully here, but in any life of Francis they ought at least to have been asked; we have a suspicion that if they were answered, we should suddenly find that much of the enigma of this sullen time of ours was answered also. So it was with the monks. The two great parties in human affairs are only the party which sees life black against white, and the party which sees it white against black, the party which macerates and blackens itself with sacrifice because the background is full of the blaze of an universal mercy, and the party which crowns itself with flowers and lights itself with bridal torches because it stands against a black curtain of incalculable night. The revellers are old, and the monks are young. It was the monks who were the spendthrifts of happiness, and we who are its misers.

Doubtless, as is apparent from Mr. Adderley's book, the clear and tranquil life of the Three Vows had a fine and delicate effect on the genius of Francis. He was primarily a poet. The perfection of his literary instinct is shown in his naming the fire "brother," and the water "sister," in the quaint demagogic dexterity of the appeal in the sermon to the fishes "that they alone were saved in the Flood." In the amazingly minute and graphic dramatisation of the life, disappointments, and excuses of any shrub or beast that he happened to be addressing, his genius has a curious resemblance to that of Burns. But if he avoided the weakness of Burns' verses to animals, the occasional morbidity, bombast, and moralisation on himself, the credit is surely due to a cleaner and more transparent life.

The general attitude of St. Francis, like that of his Master, embodied a kind of terrible common sense. The famous remark of the Caterpillar in "Alice in Wonderland"—"Why not?" impresses us as his general motto. He could not see why he should not be on good terms with all things. The pomp of war and ambition, the great empire of the Middle Ages, and all its fellows begin to look tawdry and top-heavy, under the rationality of that innocent stare. His questions were blasting and devastating, like the questions of a child. He would not have been afraid even of the nightmares of cosmogony, for he had no fear in him. To him the world was small, not because he had any views as to its size, but for the reason that gossiping ladies find it small, because so many relatives were to be found in it. If you had taken him to the loneliest star that the madness of an astronomer can conceive, he would have only beheld in it the features of a new friend.

ROSTAND

When "Cyrano de Bergerac" was published, it bore the subordinate title of a heroic comedy. We have no tradition in English literature which would justify us in calling a comedy heroic, though there was once a poet who called a comedy divine. By the current modern conception, the hero has his place in a tragedy, and the one kind of strength which is systematically denied to him is the strength to succeed. That the power of a man's spirit might possibly go to the length of turning a tragedy into a comedy is not admitted; nevertheless, almost all the primitive legends of the world are comedies, not only in the sense that they have a happy ending, but in the sense that they are based upon a certain optimistic assumption that the hero is destined to be the destroyer of the monster. Singularly enough, this modern idea of the essential disastrous character of life, when seriously considered, connects itself with a hyper-æsthetic view of tragedy and comedy which is largely due to the influence of modern France, from which the great heroic comedies of Monsieur Rostand have come. The French genius has an instinct for remedying its own evil work, and France gives always the best cure for "Frenchiness." The idea of comedy which is held in England by the school which pays most attention to the technical niceties of art is a view which renders such an idea as that of heroic comedy quite impossible. The fundamental conception in the minds of the majority of our younger writers is that comedy is, *par excellence*, a fragile thing. It is conceived to be a conventional world of the most absolutely delicate and gimcrack description. Such stories as Mr. Max Beerbohm's "Happy Hypocrite" are conceptions which would vanish or fall into utter nonsense if viewed by one single degree too seriously. But great comedy, the comedy of Shakespeare or Sterne, not only can be, but must be, taken seriously. There is nothing to which a man must give himself up with more faith and self-abandonment than to genuine laughter. In such comedies one laughs with the heroes, and not at them. The humour which steeps the stories of Falstaff and Uncle Toby is a cosmic and philosophic humour, a geniality which goes down to the depths. It is not superficial reading, it is not even, strictly speaking, light reading. Our sympathies are as much committed to the characters as if they were the predestined victims in a Greek tragedy. The modern writer of comedies may be said to boast of the brittleness of his characters. He seems always on the eve of knocking his puppets to pieces. When John Oliver Hobbes wrote for the first time a comedy of serious emotions, she named it, with a thinly-disguised contempt for her own work, "A Sentimental Comedy." The ground of this conception of the artificiality of comedy is a profound pessimism. Life in the eyes of these mournful buffoons is itself an utterly tragic thing; comedy must be as hollow as a grinning mask. It is a refuge from the world, and not even, properly speaking, a part of it. Their wit is a thin sheet of shining ice over the eternal waters of bitterness.

"Cyrano de Bergerac" came to us as the new decoration of an old truth, that merriment was one of the world's natural flowers, and not one of its exotics. The gigantesque levity, the flamboyant eloquence, the Rabelaisian puns and digressions were seen to be once more what they had been in Rabelais, the mere outbursts of a human sympathy and bravado as old and solid as the stars. The human spirit demanded wit as headlong and haughty as its will. All was expressed in the words of Cyrano at his highest moment of happiness, *Il me faut des géants*. An essential aspect of this question of heroic comedy is the question of drama in rhyme. There is nothing that affords so easy a point of attack for the dramatic realist as the conduct of a play in verse. According to his canons, it is indeed absurd to represent a number of characters facing some terrible crisis in their lives by capping rhymes like a party playing *bouts rimés*. In his eyes it must appear somewhat ridiculous that two enemies taunting each other with insupportable insults should obligingly provide each other with metrical spacing and neat and convenient rhymes. But the whole of this view rests finally upon the fact that few persons, if any, today understand what is meant by a poetical play. It is a singular thing that those poetical plays which are now written in England by the most advanced students of the drama follow exclusively the lines of Maeterlinck, and use verse and rhyme for the adornment of a profoundly tragic theme. But rhyme has a supreme appropriateness for the treatment of the higher comedy. The land of heroic comedy is, as it were, a paradise of lovers, in which it is not difficult to imagine that men could talk poetry all day long. It is far more conceivable that men's speech should flower naturally into these harmonious forms, when they are filled with the essential spirit of youth, than when they are sitting gloomily in the presence of immemorial destiny. The great error consists in supposing that poetry is an unnatural form of language. We should all like to speak poetry at the moment when we truly live, and if we do not speak, it is because we have an impediment in our speech. It is not song that is the narrow or artificial thing, it is conversation that is a broken and stammering attempt at song. When we see men in a spiritual extravaganza, like "Cyrano de Bergerac," speaking in rhyme, it is not our language disguised or distorted, but our language rounded and made whole. Rhymes answer each other as the sexes in flowers and in humanity answer each other. Men do not speak so, it is true. Even when they are inspired or in love they talk inanities. But the poetic comedy does not misrepresent the speech one half so much as the speech misrepresents the soul. Monsieur Rostand showed even more than his usual insight when he called "Cyrano de Bergerac" a comedy, despite the fact that, strictly speaking, it ends with disappointment and death. The essence of tragedy is a spiritual breakdown or decline, and in the great French play the spiritual sentiment mounts unceasingly until the last line. It is not the facts themselves, but our feeling about them, that makes tragedy and comedy, and death is more joyful in Rostand than life in Maeterlinck. The same apparent contradiction holds good in the case of the drama of "L'Aiglon," now being performed with so much success. Although the hero is a weakling, the subject a fiasco, the end a premature death and a personal disillusionment, yet, in spite of this theme, which might have been chosen for its depressing qualities, the unconquerable pæan of the praise of things, the ungovernable gaiety of the poet's song swells so high that at the end it seems to drown all the weak voices of the characters in one crashing chorus of great things and great men. A multitude of mottoes might be taken from the play to indicate and illustrate, not only its own spirit, but much of the spirit of modern life. When in the vision of the field of Wagram the horrible voices of the wounded cry out, *Les corbeaux, les corbeaux*, the Duke, overwhelmed with a nightmare of hideous trivialities, cries out, *Où, où, sont les aigles?* That antithesis might stand alone as an invocation at the beginning of the twentieth century to the spirit of heroic comedy. When an ex-General of Napoleon is asked his reason for having betrayed the Emperor, he replies, *La fatigue*, and at that a veteran private of the Great Army rushes forward, and crying passionately, *Et nous?* pours out a terrible description of the life lived by the commoner soldier. To-day, when pessimism is almost as much a symbol of wealth and fashion as jewels or cigars, when the pampered heirs of the ages can sum up life in few other words but *la fatigue*, there might surely come a cry from the vast mass of common humanity from the beginning—*et nous?* It is this potentiality for enthusiasm among the mass of men that makes the function of comedy at once common and sublime. Shakespeare's "Much Ado About Nothing" is a great comedy, because behind it is the whole pressure of that love of love which is the youth of the world, which is common to all the young, especially to those who swear they will die bachelors and old maids. "Love's Labour's Lost" is filled with the same energy, and there it falls even more definitely into the scope of our subject, since it is a comedy in rhyme in which all men speak lyrically as naturally as the birds sing in pairing time. What the love of love is to the Shakespearean comedies, that other and more mysterious human passion, the love of death, is to "L'Aiglon." Whether we shall ever have in England a new tradition of poetic comedy it is difficult at present to say, but we shall assuredly never have it until we realise that comedy is built upon everlasting foundations in the nature of things, that it is not a thing too light to capture, but too deep to plumb. Monsieur Rostand, in his description of the Battle of Wagram, does not shrink from bringing about the Duke's ears the frightful voices of actual battle, of men torn by crows, and suffocated with blood, but when the Duke, terrified at these dreadful appeals, asks them for their final word, they all cry together *Vive l'Empereur!* Monsieur Rostand, perhaps, did not know that he was writing an allegory. To me that field of Wagram is the field of the modern war of literature. We hear nothing but the voices of pain; the whole is one phonograph of horror. It is right that we should hear these things, it is right that not one of them should be silenced; but these cries of distress are not in life, as they are in modern art, the only voices; they are the voices of men, but not the voice of man. When questioned finally and seriously as to their conception of their destiny, men have from the beginning of time answered in a thousand philosophies and religions with a single voice and in a sense most sacred and tremendous, *Vive l'Empereur.*

CHARLES II.

There are a great many bonds which still connect us with Charles II., one of the idlest men of one of the idlest epochs. Among other things Charles II. represented one thing which is very rare and very satisfying; he was a real and consistent sceptic. Scepticism, both in its advantages and disadvantages, is greatly misunderstood in our time. There is a curious idea abroad that scepticism has some connection with such theories as materialism and atheism and secularism. This is of course a mistake; the true sceptic has nothing to do with these theories simply because they are theories. The true sceptic is as much a spiritualist as he is a materialist. He thinks that the savage dancing round an African idol stands quite as good a chance of being right as Darwin. He thinks that mysticism is every bit as rational as rationalism. He has indeed the most profound doubts as to whether St. Matthew wrote his own gospel. But he has quite equally profound doubts as to whether the tree he is looking at is a tree and not a rhinoceros.

This is the real meaning of that mystery which appears so prominently in the lives of great sceptics, which appears with especial prominence in the life of Charles II. I mean their constant oscillation between atheism and Roman Catholicism. Roman Catholicism is indeed a great and fixed and formidable system, but so is atheism. Atheism is indeed the most daring of all dogmas, more daring than the vision of a palpable day of judgment. For it is the assertion of a universal negative; for a man to say that there is no God in the universe is like saying that there are no insects in any of the stars.

Thus it was with that wholesome and systematic sceptic, Charles II. When he took the Sacrament according to the forms of the Roman Church in his last hour he was acting consistently as a philosopher. The wafer might not be God; similarly it might not be a wafer. To the genuine and poetical sceptic the whole world is incredible, with its bulbous mountains and its fantastic trees. The whole order of things is as outrageous as any miracle which could presume to violate it. Transubstantiation might be a dream, but if it was, it was assuredly a dream within a dream. Charles II. sought to guard himself against hell fire because he could not think hell itself more fantastic than the world as it was revealed by science. The priest crept up the staircase, the doors were closed, the few of the faithful who were present hushed themselves respectfully, and so, with every circumstance of secrecy and sanctity, with the cross uplifted and the prayers poured out, was consummated the last great act of logical unbelief.

The problem of Charles II. consists in this, that he has scarcely a moral virtue to his name, and yet he attracts us morally. We feel that some of the virtues have been dropped out in the lists made by all the saints and sages, and that Charles II. was pre-eminently successful in these wild and unmentionable virtues. The real truth of this matter and the real relation of Charles II. to the moral ideal is worth somewhat more exhaustive study.

It is a commonplace that the Restoration movement can only be understood when considered as a reaction against Puritanism. But it is insufficiently realised that the tyranny which half frustrated all the good work of Puritanism was of a very peculiar kind. It was not the fire of Puritanism, the exultation in sobriety, the frenzy of a restraint, which passed away; that still burns in the heart of England, only to be quenched by the final overwhelming sea. But it is seldom remembered that the Puritans were in their day emphatically intellectual bullies, that they relied swaggeringly on the logical necessity of Calvinism, that they bound omnipotence itself in the chains of syllogism. The Puritans fell, through the damning fact that they had a complete theory of life, through the eternal paradox that a satisfactory explanation can never satisfy. Like Brutus and the logical Romans, like the logical French Jacobins, like the logical English utilitarians, they taught the lesson that men's wants have always been right and their arguments always wrong. Reason is always a kind of brute force; those who appeal to the head rather than the heart, however pallid and polite, are necessarily men of violence. We speak of "touching" a man's heart, but we can do nothing to his head but hit it. The tyranny of the Puritans over the bodies of men was comparatively a trifle; pikes, bullets, and conflagrations are comparatively a trifle. Their real tyranny was the tyranny of aggressive reason over the cowed and demoralised human spirit. Their brooding and raving can be forgiven, can in truth be loved and reverenced, for it is humanity on fire; hatred can be genial, madness can be homely. The Puritans fell, not because they were fanatics, but because they were rationalists.

When we consider these things, when we remember that Puritanism, which means in our day a moral and almost temperamental attitude, meant in that day a singularly arrogant logical attitude, we shall comprehend a little more the grain of good that lay in the vulgarity and triviality of the Restoration. The Restoration, of which Charles II. was a pre-eminent type, was in part a revolt of all the chaotic and unclassed parts of human nature, the parts that are left over, and will always be left over, by every rationalistic system of life. This does not merely account for the revolt of the vices and of that empty recklessness and horseplay which is sometimes more irritating than any vice. It accounts also for the return of the virtue of politeness, for that also is a nameless thing ignored by logical codes. Politeness has indeed about it something mystical; like religion, it is everywhere understood and nowhere defined. Charles is not entirely to be despised because, as the type of this movement, he let himself float upon this new tide of politeness. There was some moral and social value in his perfection in little things. He could not keep the Ten Commandments, but he kept the ten thousand commandments. His name is unconnected with any great acts of duty or sacrifice, but it is connected with a great many of those acts of magnanimous politeness, of a kind of dramatic delicacy, which lie on the dim borderland between morality and art. "Charles II.," said Thackeray, with unerring brevity, "was a rascal, but not a snob." Unlike George IV. he was a gentleman, and a gentleman is a man who obeys strange statutes, not to be found in any moral text-book, and practises strange virtues nameless from the beginning of the world.

So much may be said and should be said for the Restoration, that it was the revolt of something human, if only the debris of human nature. But more cannot be said. It was emphatically a fall and not an ascent, a recoil and not an advance, a sudden weakness and not a sudden strength. That the bow of human nature was by Puritanism bent immeasurably too far, that it overstrained the soul by stretching it to the height of an almost horrible idealism, makes the collapse of the Restoration infinitely more excusable, but it does not make it any the less a collapse. Nothing can efface the essential distinction that Puritanism was one of the world's great efforts after the discovery of the true order, whereas it was the essence of the Restoration that it involved no effort at all. It is true that the Restoration was not, as has been widely assumed, the most immoral epoch of our history. Its vices cannot compare for a moment in this respect with the monstrous tragedies and almost suffocating secrecies and villainies of the Court of James I. But the dram-drinking and nose-slitting of the saturnalia of Charles II. seem at once more human and more detestable than the passions and poisons of the Renaissance, much in the same way that a monkey appears inevitably more human and more detestable than a tiger. Compared with the Renaissance, there is something Cockney about the Restoration. Not only was it too indolent for great morality, it was too indolent even for great art. It lacked that seriousness which is needed even for the pursuit of pleasure, that discipline which is essential even to a game of lawn tennis. It would have appeared to Charles II.'s poets quite as arduous to write "Paradise Lost" as to regain Paradise.

All old and vigorous languages abound in images and metaphors, which, though lightly and casually used, are in truth poems in themselves, and poems of a high and striking order. Perhaps no phrase is so terribly significant as the phrase "killing time." It is a tremendous and poetical image, the image of a kind of cosmic parricide. There are on the earth a race of revellers who do, under all their exuberance, fundamentally regard time as an enemy. Of these were Charles II. and the men of the Restoration. Whatever may have been their merits, and as we have said we think that they had merits, they can never have a place among the great representatives of the joy of life, for they belonged to those lower epicureans who kill time, as opposed to those higher epicureans who make time live.

Of a people in this temper Charles II. was the natural and rightful head. He may have been a pantomime King, but he was a King, and with all his geniality he let nobody forget it. He was not, indeed, the aimless flaneur that he has been represented. He was a patient and cunning politician, who disguised his wisdom under so perfect a mask of folly that he not only deceived his allies and opponents, but has deceived almost all the historians that have come after him. But if Charles was, as he emphatically was, the only Stuart who really achieved despotism, it was greatly due to the temper of the nation and the age. Despotism is the easiest of all governments, at any rate for the governed.

It is indeed a form of slavery, and it is the despot who is the slave. Men in a state of decadence employ professionals to fight for them, professionals to dance for them, and a professional to rule them.

Almost all the faces in the portraits of that time look, as it were, like masks put on artificially with the perruque. A strange unreality broods over the period. Distracted as we are with civic mysteries and problems we can afford to rejoice. Our tears are less desolate than their laughter, our restraints are larger than their liberty.

STEVENSON[1]

A recent incident has finally convinced us that Stevenson was, as we suspected, a great man. We knew from recent books that we have noticed, from the scorn of "Ephemera Critica" and Mr. George Moore, that Stevenson had the first essential qualification of a great man: that of being misunderstood by his opponents. But from the book which Messrs. Chatto & Windus have issued, in the same binding as Stevenson's works, "Robert Louis Stevenson," by Mr. H. Bellyse Baildon, we learn that he has the other essential qualification, that of being misunderstood by his admirers. Mr. Baildon has many interesting things to tell us about Stevenson himself, whom he knew at college. Nor are his criticisms by any means valueless. That upon the plays, especially "Beau Austin," is remarkably thoughtful and true. But it is a very singular fact, and goes far, as we say, to prove that Stevenson had that unfathomable quality which belongs to the great, that this admiring student of Stevenson can number and marshal all the master's work and distribute praise and blame with decision and even severity, without ever thinking for a moment of the principles of art and ethics which would have struck us as the very things that Stevenson nearly killed himself to express.

Mr. Baildon, for example, is perpetually lecturing Stevenson for his "pessimism"; surely a strange charge against a man who has done more than any modern artist to make men ashamed of their shame of life. But he complains that, in "The Master of Ballantrae" and "Dr. Jekyll and Mr. Hyde," Stevenson gives evil a final victory over good. Now if there was one point that Stevenson more constantly and passionately emphasised than any other it was that we must worship good for its own value and beauty, without any reference whatever to victory or failure in space and

---

1   "Robert Louis Stevenson: A Life Study in Criticism." By H. Bellyse Baildon. Chatto & Windus.

time. "Whatever we are intended to do," he said, "we are not intended to succeed." That the stars in their courses fight against virtue, that humanity is in its nature a forlorn hope, this was the very spirit that through the whole of Stevenson's work sounded a trumpet to all the brave. The story of Henry Durie is dark enough, but could anyone stand beside the grave of that sodden monomaniac and not respect him? It is strange that men should see sublime inspiration in the ruins of an old church and see none in the ruins of a man.

The author has most extraordinary ideas about Stevenson's tales of blood and spoil; he appears to think that they prove Stevenson to have had (we use Mr. Baildon's own phrase) a kind of "homicidal mania." "He [Stevenson] arrives pretty much at the paradox that one can hardly be better employed than in taking life." Mr. Baildon might as well say that Dr. Conan Doyle delights in committing inexplicable crimes, that Mr. Clark Russell is a notorious pirate, and that Mr. Wilkie Collins thought that one could hardly be better employed than in stealing moonstones and falsifying marriage registers. But Mr. Baildon is scarcely alone in this error: few people have understood properly the goriness of Stevenson. Stevenson was essentially the robust schoolboy who draws skeletons and gibbets in his Latin grammar. It was not that he took pleasure in death, but that he took pleasure in life, in every muscular and emphatic action of life, even if it were an action that took the life of another.

Let us suppose that one gentleman throws a knife at another gentleman and pins him to the wall. It is scarcely necessary to remark that there are in this transaction two somewhat varying personal points of view. The point of view of the man pinned is the tragic and moral point of view, and this Stevenson showed clearly that he understood in such stories as "The Master of Ballantrae" and "Weir of Hermiston." But there is another view of the matter—that in which the whole act is an abrupt and brilliant explosion of bodily vitality, like breaking a rock with a blow of a hammer, or just clearing a five-barred gate. This is the standpoint of romance, and it is the soul of "Treasure Island" and "The Wrecker." It was not, indeed, that Stevenson loved men less, but that he loved clubs and pistols more. He had, in truth, in the devouring universalism of his soul, a positive love for inanimate objects such as has not been known since St. Francis called the sun brother and the well sister. We feel that he was actually in love with the wooden crutch that Silver sent hurtling in the sunlight, with the box that Billy Bones left at the "Admiral Benbow," with the knife that Wicks drove through his own hand and the table. There is always in his work a certain clean-cut angularity which makes us remember that he was fond of cutting wood with an axe.

Stevenson's new biographer, however, cannot make any allowance for this deep-rooted poetry of mere sight and touch. He is always imputing something to Stevenson as a crime which Stevenson really professed as an object. He says of that glorious riot of horror, "The Destroying Angel," in "The Dynamiter," that it is "highly fantastic and putting a strain on our credulity." This is rather like describing the travels of Baron Munchausen as "unconvincing." The whole story of "The Dynamiter" is a kind of humorous nightmare, and even in that story "The Destroying Angel" is supposed to be an extravagant lie made up on the spur of the moment. It is a dream within a dream, and to accuse it of improbability is like accusing the sky of being blue. But Mr. Baildon, whether from hasty reading or natural difference of taste, cannot in the least comprehend that rich and romantic irony of Stevenson's London stories. He actually says of that portentous monument of humour, Prince Florizel of Bohemia, that, "though evidently admired by his creator, he is to me on the whole rather an irritating presence." From this we are almost driven to believe (though desperately and against our will) that Mr. Baildon thinks that Prince Florizel is to be taken seriously, as if he were a man in real life. For ourselves. Prince Florizel is almost our favourite character in fiction; but we willingly add the proviso that if we met him in real life we should kill him.

The fact is, that the whole mass of Stevenson's spiritual and intellectual virtues have been partly frustrated by one additional virtue—that of artistic dexterity. If he had chalked up his great message on a wall, like Walt Whitman, in large and straggling letters, it would have startled men like a blasphemy. But he wrote his light-headed paradoxes in so flowing a copy-book hand that everyone supposed they must be copy-book sentiments. He suffered from his versatility, not, as is loosely said, by not doing every department well enough, but by doing every department too well. As child, cockney, pirate, or Puritan, his disguises were so good that most people could not see the same man under all. It is an unjust fact that if a man can play the fiddle, give legal opinions, and black boots just tolerably, he is called an Admirable Crichton, but if he does all three thoroughly well, he is apt to be regarded, in the several departments, as a common fiddler, a common lawyer, and a common boot-black. This is what has happened in the case of Stevenson. If "Dr. Jekyll," "The Master of Ballantrae," "The Child's Garden of Verses," and "Across the Plains" had been each of them one shade less perfectly done than they were, everyone would have seen that they were all parts of the same message; but by succeeding in the proverbial miracle of being in five places at once, he has naturally convinced others that he was five different people. But the real message of Stevenson was as simple as that of Mohamet, as moral as that of Dante, as confident as that of Whitman, and as practical as that of James Watt. The conception which unites the whole varied work of Stevenson was that romance, or the vision of the possibilities of things, was far more important than mere occurrences: that one was the soul of our life, the other the body, and that the soul was the precious thing. The germ of all his stories lies in the idea that every landscape or scrap of scenery has a soul: and that soul is a story. Standing before a stunted orchard with a broken stone wall, we may know as a mere fact that no one has been through it but an elderly female cook. But everything exists in the human soul: that orchard grows in our own brain, and there it is the shrine and theatre of some strange chance between a girl and a ragged poet and a mad farmer. Stevenson stands for the conception that ideas are the real incidents: that our fancies are our adventures. To think of a cow with wings is essentially to have met one. And this is the reason for his wide diversities of narrative: he had to make one story as rich as a ruby sunset, another as grey as a hoary monolith: for the story was the soul, or rather the meaning, of the bodily vision. It is quite inappropriate to judge "The Teller of Tales" (as the Samoans called him) by the particular novels he wrote, as one would judge Mr. George Moore by "Esther Waters." These novels were only the two or three of his soul's adventures that he happened to tell. But he died with a thousand stories in his heart.

THOMAS CARLYLE

There are two main moral necessities for the work of a great man: the first is that he should believe in the truth of his message; the second is that he should believe in the acceptability of his message. It was the whole tragedy of Carlyle that he had the first and not the second.

The ordinary capital, however, which is made out of Carlyle's alleged gloom is a very paltry matter. Carlyle had his faults, both as a man and as a writer, but the attempt to explain his gospel in terms of his "liver" is merely pitiful. If indigestion invariably resulted in a "Sartor Resartus," it would be a vastly more tolerable thing than it is. Diseases do not turn into poems; even the decadent really writes with the healthy part of his organism. If Carlyle's private faults and literary virtues ran somewhat in the same line, he is only in the situation of every man; for every one of us it is surely very difficult to say precisely where our honest opinions end and our personal predilections begin. But to attempt to denounce Carlyle as a mere savage egotist cannot arise from anything but a pure inability to grasp Carlyle's gospel. "Ruskin," says a critic, "did, all the same, verily believe in God; Carlyle believed only in himself." This is certainly a distinction between the author he has understood and the author he has not understood. Carlyle believed in himself, but he could not have believed in himself more than Ruskin did; they both believed in God, because they felt that if everything else fell into wrack and ruin, themselves were permanent witnesses to God. Where they both failed was not in belief in God or in belief in themselves; they failed in belief in other people. It is not enough for a prophet to believe in his message; he must believe in its acceptability. Christ, St. Francis, Bunyan, Wesley, Mr. Gladstone, Walt Whitman, men of indescribable variety, were all alike in a certain faculty of treating the average man as their equal, of trusting to his reason and good feeling without fear and without condescension. It was this simplicity of confidence, not only in God, but in the image of God, that was lacking in Carlyle.

But the attempts to discredit Carlyle's religious sentiment must absolutely fall to the ground. The profound security of Carlyle's sense of the unity of the Cosmos is like that of a Hebrew prophet; and it has the same expression that it had in the Hebrew prophets—humour. A man must be very full of faith to jest about his divinity. No Neo-Pagan delicately suggesting a revival of Dionysus, no vague, half converted Theosophist groping towards a recognition of Buddha, would ever think of cracking jokes on the matter. But to the Hebrew prophets their religion was so solid a thing, like a mountain or a mammoth, that the irony of its contact with trivial and fleeting matters struck them like a blow. So it was with Carlyle. His supreme contribution, both to philosophy and literature, was his sense of the sarcasm of eternity. Other writers had seen the hope or the terror of the heavens, he alone saw the humour of them. Other writers had seen that there could be something elemental and eternal in a song or statute, he alone saw that there could be something elemental and eternal in a joke. No one who ever read it will forget the passage, full of dark and agnostic gratification, in which he narrates that some Court chronicler described Louis XV. as "falling asleep in the Lord." "Enough for us that he did fall asleep; that, curtained in thick night, under what keeping we ask not, he at least will never, through unending ages, insult the face of the sun any more ... and we go on, if not to better forms of beastliness, at least to fresher ones."

The supreme value of Carlyle to English literature was that he was the founder of modern irrationalism; a movement fully as important as modern rationalism. A great deal is said in these days about the value or valuelessness of logic. In the main, indeed, logic is not a productive tool so much as a weapon of defence. A man building up an intellectual system has to build like Nehemiah, with the sword in one hand and the trowel in the other. The imagination, the constructive quality, is the trowel, and argument is the sword. A wide experience of actual intellectual affairs will lead most people to the conclusion that logic is mainly valuable as a weapon wherewith to exterminate logicians.

But though this may be true enough in practice, it scarcely clears up the position of logic in human affairs. Logic is a machine of the mind, and if it is used honestly it ought to bring out an honest conclusion. When people say that you can prove anything by logic, they are not using words in a fair sense. What they mean is that you can prove anything by bad logic. Deep in the mystic ingratitude of the soul of man there is an extraordinary tendency to use the name for an organ, when what is meant is the abuse or decay of that organ. Thus we speak of a man suffering from "nerves," which is about as sensible as talking about a man suffering from ten fingers. We speak of "liver" and "digestion" when we mean the failure of liver and the absence of digestion. And in the same manner we speak of the dangers of logic, when what we really mean is the danger of fallacy.

But the real point about the limitation of logic and the partial overthrow of logic by writers like Carlyle is deeper and somewhat different. The fault of the great mass of logicians is not that they bring out a false result, or, in other words, are not logicians at all. Their fault is that by an inevitable psychological habit they tend to forget that there are two parts of a logical process, the first the choosing of an assumption, and the second the arguing upon it, and humanity, if it devotes itself too persistently to the study of sound reasoning, has a certain tendency to lose the faculty of sound assumption. It is astonishing how constantly one may hear from rational and even rationalistic persons such a phrase as "He did not prove the very thing with which he started," or, "The whole of his case rested upon a pure assumption," two peculiarities which may be found by the curious in the works of Euclid. It is astonishing, again, how constantly one hears rationalists arguing upon some deep topic, apparently without troubling about the deep assumptions involved, having lost their sense, as it were, of the real colour and character of a man's assumption. For instance, two men will argue about whether patriotism is a good thing and never discover until the end, if at all, that the cosmopolitan is basing his whole case upon the idea that man should, if he can, become as God, with equal sympathies and no prejudices, while the nationalist denies any such duty at the very start, and regards man as an animal who has preferences, as a bird has feathers.

Thus it was with Carlyle: he startled men by attacking not arguments, but assumptions. He simply brushed aside all the matters which the men of the nineteenth century held to be incontrovertible, and appealed directly to the very different class of matters which they knew to be true. He induced men to study less the truth of their reasoning, and more the truth of the assumptions upon which they reasoned. Even where his view was not the highest truth, it was always a refreshing and beneficent heresy. He denied every one of the postulates upon which the age of reason based itself. He denied the theory of progress which assumed that we must be better off than the people of the twelfth century. Whether we were better than the people of the twelfth century, according to him, depended entirely upon whether we chose or deserved to be.

He denied every type and species of prop or association or support which threw the responsibility upon civilisation or society, or anything but the individual conscience. He has often been called a prophet. The real ground of the truth of this phrase is often neglected. Since the last era of purely religious literature, the era of English Puritanism, there has been no writer in whose eyes the soul stood so much alone.

Carlyle was, as we have suggested, a mystic, and mysticism was with him, as with all its genuine professors, only a transcendent form of common sense. Mysticism and common sense alike consist in a sense of the dominance of certain truths and tendencies which cannot be formally demonstrated or even formally named. Mysticism and common sense are alike appeals to realities that we all know to be real, but which have no place in argument except as postulates. Carlyle's work did consist in breaking through formulæ, old and new, to these old and silent and ironical sanities. Philosophers might abolish kings a hundred times over, he maintained, they could not alter the fact that every man and woman does choose a king and repudiate all the pride of citizenship for the exultation of humility. If inequality of this kind was a weakness, it was a weakness bound up with the very strength of the universe. About hero worship, indeed, few critics have done the smallest justice to Carlyle. Misled by those hasty and choleric passages in which he sometimes expressed a preference for mere violence, passages which were a great deal more connected with his temperament than with his philosophy, they have finally imbibed the notion that Carlyle's theory of hero worship was a theory of terrified submission to stern and arrogant men. As a matter of fact, Carlyle is really inhumane about some questions, but he is never inhumane about hero worship. His view is not that human nature is so vulgar and silly a thing that it must be guided and driven; it is, on the contrary, that human nature is so chivalrous and fundamentally magnanimous a thing that even the meanest have it in them to love a leader more than themselves, and to prefer loyalty to rebellion. When he speaks of this trait in human nature Carlyle's tone invariably softens. We feel that for the moment he is kindled with admiration of mankind, and almost reaches the verge of Christianity. Whatever else was acid and captious about Carlyle's utterances, his hero worship was not only humane, it was almost optimistic. He admired great men primarily, and perhaps correctly, because he thought that they were more human than other men. The evil side of the influence of Carlyle and his religion of hero worship did not consist in the emotional worship of valour and success; that was a part of him, as, indeed, it is a part of all healthy children. Where Carlyle really did harm was in the fact that he, more than any modern man, is responsible for the increase of that modern habit of what is vulgarly called "Going the whole hog." Often in matters of passion and conquest it is a singularly hoggish hog. This remarkable modern craze for making one's philosophy, religion, politics, and temper all of a piece, of seeking in all incidents for opportunities to assert and reassert some favourite mental attitude, is a thing which existed comparatively little in other centuries. Solomon and Horace, Petrarch and Shakespeare were pessimists when they were melancholy, and optimists when they were happy. But the optimist of today seems obliged to prove that gout and unrequited love make him dance with joy, and the pessimist of today to prove that sunshine and a good supper convulse him with inconsolable anguish. Carlyle was strongly possessed with this mania for spiritual consistency. He wished to take the same view of the wars of the angels and of the paltriest riot at Donnybrook Fair. It was this species of insane logic which led him into his chief errors, never his natural enthusiasms. Let us take an example. Carlyle's defence of slavery is a thoroughly ridiculous thing, weak alike in argument and in moral instinct. The truth is, that he only took it up from the passion for applying everywhere his paradoxical defence of aristocracy. He blundered, of course, because he did not see that slavery has nothing in the world to do with aristocracy, that it is, indeed, almost its opposite. The defence which Carlyle and all its thoughtful defenders have made for aristocracy was that a few persons could more rapidly and firmly decide public affairs in the interests of the people. But slavery is not even supposed to be a government for the good of the governed. It is a possession of the governed avowedly for the good of the governors. Aristocracy uses the strong for the service of the weak; slavery uses the weak for the service of the strong. It is no derogation to man as a spiritual being, as Carlyle firmly believed he was, that he should be ruled and guided for his own good like a child—for a child who is always ruled and guided we regard as the very type of spiritual existence. But it is a derogation and an absolute contradiction to that human spirituality in which Carlyle believed that a man should be owned like a tool for someone else's good, as if he had no personal destiny in the Cosmos. We draw attention to this particular error of Carlyle's because we think that it is a curious example of the waste and unclean places into which that remarkable animal, "the whole hog," more than once led him.

In this respect Carlyle has had unquestionably long and an unquestionably bad influence. The whole of that recent political ethic which conceives that if we only go far enough we may finish a thing for once and all, that being strong consists chiefly in being deliberately deaf and blind, owes a great deal of its complete sway to his example. Out of him flows most of the philosophy of Nietzsche, who is in modern times the supreme maniac of this moonstruck consistency. Though Nietzsche and Carlyle were in reality profoundly different, Carlyle being a stiff-necked peasant and Nietzsche a very fragile aristocrat, they were alike in this one quality of which we speak, the strange and pitiful audacity with which they applied their single ethical test to everything in heaven and earth. The disciple of Nietzsche, indeed, embraces immorality like an austere and difficult faith. He urges himself to lust and cruelty with the same tremulous enthusiasm with which a Christian urges himself to purity and patience; he struggles as a monk struggles with bestial visions and temptations with the ancient necessities of honour and justice and compassion. To this madhouse, it can hardly be denied, has Carlyle's intellectual courage brought many at last.

TOLSTOY AND THE CULT OF SIMPLICITY

The whole world is certainly heading for a great simplicity, not deliberately, but rather inevitably. It is not a mere fashion of false innocence, like that of the French aristocrats before the Revolution, who built an altar to Pan, and who taxed the peasantry for the enormous expenditure which is needed in order to live the simple life of peasants. The simplicity towards which the world is driving is the necessary outcome of all our systems and speculations and of our deep and continuous contemplation of things. For the universe is like everything in it; we have to look at it repeatedly and habitually before we see it. It is only when we have seen it for the hundredth time that we see it for the first time. The more consistently things are contemplated, the more they tend to unify themselves and therefore to simplify themselves. The simplification of anything is always sensational. Thus monotheism is the most sensational of things: it is as if we gazed long at a design full of disconnected objects, and, suddenly, with a stunning thrill, they came together into a huge and staring face.

Few people will dispute that all the typical movements of our time are upon this road towards simplification. Each system seeks to be more fundamental than the other; each seeks, in the literal sense, to undermine the other. In art, for example, the old conception of man, classic as the Apollo Belvedere, has first been attacked by the realist, who asserts that man, as a fact of natural history, is a creature with colourless hair and a freckled face. Then comes the Impressionist, going yet deeper, who asserts that to his physical eye, which alone is certain, man is a creature with purple hair and a grey face. Then comes the Symbolist, and says that to his soul, which alone is certain, man is a creature with green hair and a blue face. And all the great writers of our time represent in one form or another this attempt to reestablish communication with the elemental, or, as it is sometimes more roughly and fallaciously expressed, to return to nature. Some think that the return to nature consists in drinking no wine; some think that it consists in drinking a great deal more than is good for them. Some think that the return to nature is achieved by beating swords into ploughshares; some think it is achieved by turning ploughshares into very ineffectual British War Office bayonets. It is natural, according to the Jingo, for a man to kill other people with gunpowder and himself with gin. It is natural, according to the humanitarian revolutionist, to kill other people with dynamite and himself with vegetarianism. It would be too obviously Philistine a sentiment, perhaps, to suggest that the claim of either of these persons to be obeying the voice of nature is interesting when we consider that they require huge volumes of paradoxical argument to persuade themselves or anyone else of the truth of their conclusions. But the giants of our time are undoubtedly alike in that they approach by very different roads this conception of the return to simplicity. Ibsen returns to nature by the angular exterior of fact, Maeterlinck by the eternal tendencies of fable. Whitman returns to nature by seeing how much he can accept, Tolstoy by seeing how much he can reject.

Now, this heroic desire to return to nature, is, of course, in some respects, rather like the heroic desire of a kitten to return to its own tail. A tail is a simple and beautiful object, rhythmic in curve and soothing in texture; but it is certainly one of the minor but characteristic qualities of a tail that it should hang behind. It is impossible to deny that it would in some degree lose its character if attached to any other part of the anatomy. Now, nature is like a tail in the sense that it vitally important, if it is to discharge its real duty, that it should be always behind. To imagine that we can see nature, especially our own nature, face to face, is a folly; it is even a blasphemy. It is like the conduct of a cat in some mad fairy-tale, who should set out on his travels with the firm conviction that he would find his tail growing like a tree in the meadows at the end of the world. And the actual effect of the travels of the philosopher in search of nature, when seen from the outside, looks very like the gyrations of the tail-pursuing kitten, exhibiting much enthusiasm but little dignity, much cry and very little tail. The grandeur of nature is that she is omnipotent and unseen, that she is perhaps ruling us most when we think that she is heeding us least. "Thou art a God that hidest Thyself," said the Hebrew poet. It may be said with all reverence that it is behind a man's back that the spirit of nature hides.

It is this consideration that lends a certain air of futility even to all the inspired simplicities and thunderous veracities of Tolstoy. We feel that a man cannot make himself simple merely by warring on complexity; we feel, indeed, in our saner moments, that a man cannot make himself simple at all. A self-conscious simplicity may well be far more intrinsically ornate than luxury itself. Indeed, a great deal of the pomp and sumptuousness of the world's history was simple in the truest sense. It was born of an almost babyish receptiveness; it was the work of men who had eyes to wonder and men who had ears to hear.

> *"King Solomon brought merchant men*
> *Because of his desire*
> *With peacocks, apes, and ivory,*
> *From Tarshish unto Tyre."*

But this proceeding was not a part of the wisdom of Solomon; it was a part of his folly—I had almost said of his innocence. Tolstoy, we feel, would not be content with hurling satire and denunciation at "Solomon in all his glory." With fierce and unimpeachable logic he would go a step further. He would spend days and nights in the meadows stripping the shameless crimson coronals off the lilies of the field.

The new collection of "Tales from Tolstoy," translated and edited by Mr. R. Nisbet Bain, is calculated to draw particular attention to this ethical and ascetic side of Tolstoy's work. In one sense, and that the deepest sense, the work of Tolstoy is, of course, a genuine and noble appeal to simplicity. The narrow notion that an artist may not teach is pretty well exploded by now. But the truth of the matter is, that an artist teaches far more by his mere background and properties, his landscape, his costume, his idiom and technique—all the part of his work, in short, of which he is probably entirely unconscious, than by the elaborate and pompous moral dicta which he fondly imagines to be his opinions. The real distinction between the ethics of high art and the ethics of manufactured and didactic art lies in the simple fact that the bad fable has a moral, while the good fable is a moral. And the real moral of Tolstoy comes out constantly in these stories, the great moral which lies at the heart of all his work, of which he is probably unconscious, and of which it is quite likely that he would vehemently disapprove. The curious cold white light of morning that shines over all the tales, the folklore simplicity with which "a man or a woman" are spoken of without further identification, the love—one might almost say the lust—for the qualities of brute materials, the hardness of wood, and the softness of mud, the ingrained belief in a certain ancient kindliness sitting beside the very cradle of the race of man—these influences are truly moral. When we put beside them the trumpeting and tearing nonsense of the didactic Tolstoy, screaming for an obscene purity, shouting for an inhuman peace, hacking up human life into small sins with a chopper, sneering at men, women, and children out of respect to humanity, combining in one chaos of contradictions an unmanly Puritan and an uncivilised prig, then, indeed, we scarcely know whither Tolstoy has vanished. We know not what to do with this small and noisy moralist who is inhabiting one corner of a great and good man.

It is difficult in every case to reconcile Tolstoy the great artist with Tolstoy the almost venomous reformer. It is difficult to believe that a man who draws in such noble outlines the dignity of the daily life of humanity regards as evil that divine act of procreation by which that dignity is renewed from age to age. It is difficult to believe that a man who has painted with so frightful an honesty the heartrending emptiness of the life of the poor can really grudge them every one of their pitiful pleasures, from courtship to tobacco. It is difficult to believe that a poet in prose who has so powerfully exhibited the earth-born air of man, the essential kinship of a human being, with the landscape in which he lives, can deny so elemental a virtue as that which attaches a man to his own ancestors and his own land. It is difficult to believe that the man who feels so poignantly the detestable insolence of oppression would not actually, if he had the chance, lay the oppressor flat with his fist. All, however, arises from the search after a false simplicity, the aim of being, if I may so express it, more natural than it is natural to be. It would not only be more human, it would be more humble of us to be content to be complex. The truest kinship with humanity would lie in doing as humanity has always done, accepting with a sportsmanlike relish the estate to which we are called, the star of our happiness, and the fortunes of the land of our birth.

The work of Tolstoy has another and more special signifi-
cance. It represents the re-assertion of a certain awful common
sense which characterised the most extreme utterances of Christ.
It is true that we cannot turn the cheek to the smiter; it is true that
we cannot give our cloak to the robber; civilisation is too complicated, too vain-glorious, too emotional. The robber would brag,
and we should blush; in other words, the robber and we are alike
sentimentalists. The command of Christ is impossible, but it is not
insane; it is rather sanity preached to a planet of lunatics. If the
whole world was suddenly stricken with a sense of humour it
would find itself mechanically fulfilling the Sermon on the
Mount. It is not the plain facts of the world which stand in the way
of that consummation, but its passions of vanity and self-adver-
tisement and morbid sensibility. It is true that we cannot turn the
cheek to the smiter, and the sole and sufficient reason is that we
have not the pluck. Tolstoy and his followers have shown that they
have the pluck, and even if we think they are mistaken, by this sign
they conquer. Their theory has the strength of an utterly consistent thing. It represents that doctrine of mildness and non-resistance which is the last and most audacious of all the forms of
resistance to every existing authority. It is the great strike of the
Quakers which is more formidable than many sanguinary revolutions. If human beings could only succeed in achieving a real pas-
sive resistance they would be strong with the appalling strength of
inanimate things, they would be calm with the maddening calm of
oak or iron, which conquer without vengeance and are conquered
without humiliation. The theory of Christian duty enunciated by
them is that we should never conquer by force, but always, if we
can, conquer by persuasion. In their mythology St. George did not
conquer the dragon: he tied a pink ribbon round its neck and gave
it a saucer of milk. According to them, a course of consistent kind-
ness to Nero would have turned him into something only faintly
represented by Alfred the Great. In fact, the policy recommended
by this school for dealing with the bovine stupidity and bovine
fury of this world is accurately summed up in the celebrated verse
of Mr. Edward Lear:

> *"There was an old man who said, 'How*
> *Shall I flee from this terrible cow?*
> *I will sit on a stile and continue to smile*

Till I soften the heart of this cow.'"

Their confidence in human nature is really honourable and magnificent; it takes the form of refusing to believe the overwhelming majority of mankind, even when they set out to explain their own motives. But although most of us would in all probability tend at first sight to consider this new sect of Christians as little less outrageous than some brawling and absurd sect in the Reformation, yet we should fall into a singular error in doing so. The Christianity of Tolstoy is, when we come to consider it, one of the most thrilling and dramatic incidents in our modern civilisation. It represents a tribute to the Christian religion more sensational than the breaking of seals or the falling of stars.

From the point of view of a rationalist, the whole world is rendered almost irrational by the single phenomenon of Christian Socialism. It turns the scientific universe topsy-turvy, and makes it essentially possible that the key of all social evolution may be found in the dusty casket of some discredited creed. It cannot be amiss to consider this phenomenon as it realty is.

The religion of Christ has, like many true things, been disproved an extraordinary number of times. It was disproved by the Neo-Platonist philosophers at the very moment when it was first starting forth upon its startling and universal career. It was disproved again by many of the sceptics of the Renaissance only a few years before its second and supremely striking embodiment, the religion of Puritanism, was about to triumph over many kings and civilise many continents. We all agree that these schools of negation were only interludes in its history; but we all believe naturally and inevitably that the negation of our own day is really a breaking up of the theological cosmos, an Armageddon, a Ragnorak, a twilight of the gods. The man of the nineteenth century, like a schoolboy of sixteen, believes that his doubt and depression are symbols of the end of the world. In our day the great irreligionists who did nothing but dethrone God and drive angels before them have been outstripped, distanced, and made to look orthodox and humdrum. A newer race of sceptics has found something infinitely more exciting to do than nailing down the lids upon a million coffins, and the body upon a single cross. They have disputed not only the elementary creeds, but the elementary laws of mankind, property, patriotism, civil obedience. They have arraigned civilisation as openly as the materialists have arraigned theology; they have damned all the philosophers even lower than they have damned the saints. Thousands of modern men move quietly and conventionally among their fellows while holding views of national limitation or landed property that would have made Voltaire shudder like a nun listening to blasphemies. And the last and wildest phase of this saturnalia of scepticism, the school that goes furthest among thousands who go so far, the school that denies the moral validity of those ideals of courage or obedience which are recognised even among pirates, this school bases itself upon the literal words of Christ, like Dr. Watts or Messrs. Moody and Sankey. Never in the whole history of the world was such a tremendous tribute paid to the vitality of an ancient creed. Compared with this, it would be a small thing if the Red Sea were cloven asunder, or the sun did stand still at midday. We are faced with the phenomenon that a set of revolutionists whose contempt for all the ideals of family and nation would evoke horror in a thieves' kitchen, who can rid themselves of those elementary instincts of the man and the gentleman which cling to the very bones of our civilisation, cannot rid themselves of the influence of two or three remote Oriental anecdotes written in corrupt Greek. The fact, when realised, has about it something stunning and hypnotic. The most convinced rationalist is in its presence suddenly stricken with a strange and ancient vision, sees the immense sceptical cosmogonies of this age as dreams going the way of a thousand forgotten heresies, and believes for a moment that the dark sayings handed down through eighteen centuries may, indeed, contain in themselves the revolutions of which we have only begun to dream.

This value which we have above suggested unquestionably belongs to the Tolstoians, who may roughly be described as the new Quakers. With their strange optimism, and their almost appalling logical courage, they offer a tribute to Christianity which no orthodoxies could offer. It cannot but be remarkable to watch a revolution in which both the rulers and the rebels march under the same symbol. But the actual theory of non-resistance itself, with all its kindred theories, is not, I think, characterised by that intellectual obviousness and necessity which its supporters claim for it. A pamphlet before us shows us an extraordinary number of statements about the new Testament, of which the accuracy is by no means so striking as the confidence. To begin with, we must protest against a habit of quoting and paraphrasing at the same time. When a man is discussing what Jesus meant, let him state first of all what He said, not what the man thinks He would have said if he had expressed Himself more clearly. Here is an instance of question and answer:

> Q. "How did our Master Himself sum up the law in a few words?"
> A. "Be ye merciful, be ye perfect even as your Father; your Father in the spirit world is merciful, is perfect."

There is nothing in this, perhaps, which Christ might not have said except the abominable metaphysical modernism of "the spirit world"; but to say that it is recorded that He did say it, is like saying it is recorded that He preferred palm trees to sycamores. It is a simple and unadulterated untruth. The author should know that these words have meant a thousand things to a thousand people, and that if more ancient sects had paraphrased them as cheerfully as he, he would never have had the text upon which he founds his theory. In a pamphlet in which plain printed words cannot be left alone, it is not surprising if there are mis-statements upon larger matters. Here is a statement clearly and philosophically laid down which we can only content ourselves with flatly denying: "The fifth rule of our Lord is that we should take special pains to cultivate the same kind of regard for people of foreign countries, and for those generally who do not belong to us, or even have an antipathy to us, which we already entertain towards our own people, and those who are in sympathy with us." I should very much like to know where in the whole of the New Testament the author finds this violent, unnatural, and immoral proposition. Christ did not have the same kind of regard for one person as for another. We are specifically told that there were certain persons whom He specially loved. It is most improbable that He thought of other nations as He thought of His own. The sight of His national city moved Him to tears, and the highest compliment He paid was, "Behold an Israelite indeed." The author has simply confused two entirely distinct things. Christ commanded us to have love for all men, but even if we had equal love for all men, to speak of having the same love for all men is merely bewildering nonsense. If we love a man at all, the impression he produces on us must be vitally different to the impression produced by another man whom we love. To speak of having the same kind of regard for both is about as sensible as asking a man whether he prefers chrysanthemums or billiards. Christ did not love humanity; He never said He loved humanity; He loved men. Neither He nor anyone else can love humanity; it is like loving a gigantic centipede. And the reason that the Tolstoians can even endure to think of an equally distributed affection is that their love of humanity is a logical love, a love into which they are coerced by their own theories, a love which would be an insult to a tom-cat.

But the greatest error of all lies in the mere act of cutting up the teaching of the New Testament into five rules. It precisely and ingeniously misses the most dominant characteristic of the teaching—its absolute spontaneity. The abyss between Christ and all His modern interpreters is that we have no record that He ever wrote a word, except with His finger in the sand. The whole is the history of one continuous and sublime conversation. Thousands of rules have been deduced from it before these Tolstoian rules were made, and thousands will be deduced afterwards. It was not for any pompous proclamation, it was not for any elaborate output of printed volumes; it was for a few splendid and idle words that the cross was set up on Calvary, and the earth gaped, and the sun was darkened at noonday.

SAVONAROLA

Savonarola is a man whom we shall probably never understand until we know what horror may lie at the heart of civilisation. This we shall not know until we are civilised. It may be hoped, in one sense, that we may never understand Savonarola.

The great deliverers of men have, for the most part, saved them from calamities which we all recognise as evil, from calamities which are the ancient enemies of humanity. The great lawgivers saved us from anarchy: the great physicians saved us from pestilence: the great reformers saved us from starvation. But there is a huge and bottomless evil compared with which all these are fleabites, the most desolating curse that can fall upon men or nations, and it has no name except we call it satisfaction. Savonarola did not save men from anarchy, but from order; not from pestilence, but from paralysis; not from starvation, but from luxury. Men like Savonarola are the witnesses to the tremendous psychological fact at the back of all our brains, but for which no name has ever been found, that ease is the worst enemy of happiness, and civilisation potentially the end of man.

For I fancy that Savonarola's thrilling challenge to the luxury of his day went far deeper than the mere question of sin. The modern rationalistic admirers of Savonarola, from George Eliot downwards, dwell, truly enough, upon the sound ethical justification of Savonarola's anger, upon the hideous and extravagant character of the crimes which polluted the palaces of the Renaissance. But they need not be so anxious to show that Savonarola was no ascetic, that he merely picked out the black specks of wickedness with the priggish enlightenment of a member of an Ethical Society. Probably he did hate the civilisation of his time, and not merely its sins; and that is precisely where he was infinitely more profound than a modern moralist. He saw, that the actual crimes were not the only evils: that stolen jewels and poisoned wine and obscene pictures were merely the symptoms; that the disease was the complete dependence upon jewels and wine and pictures. This is a thing constantly forgotten in judging of ascetics and

Puritans in old times. A denunciation of harmless sports did not always mean an ignorant hatred of what no one but a narrow moralist would call harmful. Sometimes it meant an exceedingly enlightened hatred of what no one but a narrow moralist would call harmless. Ascetics are sometimes more advanced than the average man, as well as less.

Such, at least, was the hatred in the heart of Savonarola. He was making war against no trivial human sins, but against godless and thankless quiescence, against getting used to happiness, the mystic sin by which all creation fell. He was preaching that severity which is the sign-manual of youth and hope. He was preaching that alertness, that clean agility and vigilance, which is as necessary to gain pleasure as to gain holiness, as indispensable in a lover as in a monk. A critic has truly pointed out that Savonarola could not have been fundamentally anti-æsthetic, since he had such friends as Michael Angelo, Botticelli, and Luca della Robbia. The fact is that this purification and austerity are even more necessary for the appreciation of life and laughter than for anything else. To let no bird fly past unnoticed, to spell patiently the stones and weeds, to have the mind a storehouse of sunset, requires a discipline in pleasure, and an education in gratitude.

The civilisation which surrounded Savonarola on every side was a civilisation which had already taken the wrong turn, the turn that leads to endless inventions and no discoveries, in which new things grow old with confounding rapidity, but in which no old things ever grow new. The monstrosity of the crimes of the Renaissance was not a mark of imagination; it was a mark, as all monstrosity is, of the loss of imagination. It is only when a man has really ceased to see a horse as it is, that he invents a centaur, only when he can no longer be surprised at an ox, that he worships the devil. Diablerie is the stimulant of the jaded fancy; it is the dram-drinking of the artist. Savonarola addressed himself to the hardest of all earthly tasks, that of making men turn back and wonder at the simplicities they had learnt to ignore. It is strange that the most unpopular of all doctrines is the doctrine which declares the common life divine. Democracy, of which Savonarola was so fiery an exponent, is the hardest of gospels; there is nothing that so terrifies men as the decree that they are all kings. Christianity, in Savonarola's mind, identical with democracy, is the hardest of gospels; there is nothing that so strikes men with fear as the saying that they are all the sons of God.

Savonarola and his republic fell. The drug of despotism was administered to the people, and they forgot what they had been. There are some at the present day who have so strange a respect for art and letters, and for mere men of genius, that they conceive the reign of the Medici to be an improvement on that of the great Florentine republican. It is such men as these and their civilisation that we have at the present day to fear. We are surrounded on many sides by the same symptoms as those which awoke the unquenchable wrath of Savonarola—a hedonism that is more sick of happiness than an invalid is sick of pain, an art sense that seeks the assistance of crime since it has exhausted nature. In many modern works we find veiled and horrible hints of a truly Renaissance sense of the beauty of blood, the poetry of murder. The bankrupt and depraved imagination does not see that a living man is far more dramatic than a dead one. Along with this, as in the time of the Medici, goes the falling back into the arms of despotism, the hunger for the strong man which is unknown among strong men. The masterful hero is worshipped as he is worshipped by the readers of the "Bow Bells Novelettes," and for the same reason—a profound sense of personal weakness. That tendency to devolve our duties descends on us, which is the soul of slavery, alike whether for its menial tasks it employs serfs or emperors. Against all this the great clerical republican stands in everlasting protest, preferring his failure to his rival's success. The issue is still between him and Lorenzo, between the responsibilities of liberty and the license of slavery, between the perils of truth and the security of silence, between the pleasure of toil and the toil of pleasure. The supporters of Lorenzo the Magnificent are assuredly among us, men for whom even nations and empires only exist to satisfy the moment, men to whom the last hot hour of summer is better than a sharp and wintry spring. They have an art, a literature, a political philosophy, which are all alike valued for their immediate effect upon the taste, not for what they promise of the destiny of the spirit. Their statuettes and sonnets are rounded and perfect, while "Macbeth" is in comparison a fragment, and the Moses of Michael Angelo a hint. Their campaigns and battles are always called triumphant, while Cæsar and Cromwell wept for many humiliations. And the end of it all is the hell of no resistance, the hell of an unfathomable softness, until the whole nature recoils into madness and the chamber of civilisation is no longer merely a cushioned apartment, but a padded cell.

This last and worst of human miseries Savonarola saw afar off, and bent his whole gigantic energies to turning the chariot into another course. Few men understood his object; some called him a madman, some a charlatan, some an enemy of human joy. They would not even have understood if he had told them, if he had said that he was saving them from a calamity of contentment which should be the end of joys and sorrows alike. But there are those today who feel the same silent danger, and who bend themselves to the same silent resistance. They also are supposed to be contending for some trivial political scruple.

Mr. M'Hardy says, in defending Savonarola, that the number of fine works of art destroyed in the Burning of the Vanities has been much exaggerated. I confess that I hope the pile contained stacks of incomparable masterpieces if the sacrifice made that one real moment more real. Of one thing I am sure, that Savonarola's friend Michael Angelo would have piled all his own statues one on top of the other, and burnt them to ashes, if only he had been certain that the glow transfiguring the sky was the dawn of a younger and wiser world.

THE POSITION OF
SIR WALTER SCOTT

Walter Scott is a writer who should just now be re-emerging into his own high place in letters, for unquestionably the recent, though now dwindling, schools of severely technical and æsthetic criticism have been unfavourable to him. He was a chaotic and unequal writer, and if there is one thing in which artists have improved since his time, it is in consistency and equality. It would perhaps be unkind to inquire whether the level of the modern man of letters, as compared with Scott, is due to the absence of valleys or the absence of mountains. But in any case, we have learnt in our day to arrange our literary effects carefully, and the only point in which we fall short of Scott is in the incidental misfortune that we have nothing particular to arrange.

It is said that Scott is neglected by modern readers; if so, the matter could be more appropriately described by saying that modern readers are neglected by Providence. The ground of this neglect, in so far as it exists, must be found, I suppose, in the general sentiment that, like the beard of Polonius, he is too long. Yet it is surely a peculiar thing that in literature alone a house should be despised because it is too large, or a host impugned because he is too generous. If romance be really a pleasure, it is difficult to understand the modern reader's consuming desire to get it over, and if it be not a pleasure, it is difficult to understand his desire to have it at all. Mere size, it seems to me, cannot be a fault. The fault must lie in some disproportion. If some of Scott's stories are dull and dilatory, it is not because they are giants, but because they are hunchbacks or cripples. Scott was very far indeed from being a perfect writer, but I do not think that it can be shown that the large and elaborate plan on which his stories are built was by any means an imperfection. He arranged his endless prefaces and his colossal introductions just as an architect plans great gates and long approaches to a really large house. He did not share the latter-day desire to get quickly through a story. He enjoyed narrative as a sensation; he did not wish to swallow a story like a pill, that it should do him good afterwards. He desired to taste it like a glass of port, that it might do him good at the time. The reader sits late at his banquets. His characters have that air of immortality which belongs to those of Dumas and Dickens. We should not be surprised to meet them in any number of sequels. Scott, in his heart of hearts, probably would have liked to write an endless story without either beginning or close.

Walter Scott is a great, and, therefore, mysterious man. He will never be understood until Romance is understood, and that will be only when Time, Man, and Eternity are understood. To say that Scott had more than any other man that ever lived a sense of the romantic seems, in these days, a slight and superficial tribute. The whole modern theory arises from one fundamental mistake—the idea that romance is in some way a plaything with life, a figment, a conventionality, a thing upon the outside. No genuine criticism of romance will ever arise until we have grasped the fact that romance lies not upon the outside of life, but absolutely in the centre of it. The centre of every man's existence is a dream. Death, disease, insanity, are merely material accidents, like toothache or a twisted ankle. That these brutal forces always besiege and often capture the citadel does not prove that they are the citadel. The boast of the realist (applying what the reviewers call his scalpel) is that he cuts into the heart of life; but he makes a very shallow incision, if he only reaches as deep as habits and calamities and sins. Deeper than all these lies a man's vision of himself, as swaggering and sentimental as a penny novelette. The literature of can-dour unearths innumerable weaknesses and elements of lawlessness which is called romance. It perceives superficial habits like murder and dipsomania, but it does not perceive the deepest of sins—the sin of vanity—vanity which is the mother of all day-dreams and adventures, the one sin that is not shared with any boon companion, or whispered to any priest.

In estimating, therefore, the ground of Scott's pre-eminence in romance we must absolutely rid ourselves of the notion that romance or adventure are merely materialistic things involved in the tangle of a plot or the multiplicity of drawn swords. We must remember that it is, like tragedy or farce, a state of the soul, and that, for some dark and elemental reason which we can never understand, this state of the soul is evoked in us by the sight of certain places or the contemplation of certain human crises, by a stream rushing under a heavy and covered wooden bridge, or by a man plunging a knife or sword into tough timber. In the selection of these situations which catch the spirit of romance as in a net, Scott has never been equalled or even approached. His finest scenes affect us like fragments of a hilarious dream. They have the same quality which is often possessed by those nocturnal comedies—that of seeming more human than our waking life—even while they are less possible. Sir Arthur Wardour, with his daughter and the old beggar crouching in a cranny of the cliff as night falls and the tide closes around them, are actually in the coldest and bitterest of practical situations. Yet the whole incident has a quality that can only be called boyish. It is warmed with all the colours of an incredible sunset. Rob Roy trapped in the Tolbooth, and confronted with Bailie Nicol Jarvie, draws no sword, leaps from no window, affects none of the dazzling external acts upon which contemporary romance depends, yet that plain and humourous dialogue is full of the essential philosophy of romance which is an almost equal betting upon man and destiny. Perhaps the most profoundly thrilling of all Scott's situations is that in which the family of Colonel Mannering are waiting for the carriage which may or may not arrive by night to bring an unknown man into a princely possession. Yet almost the whole of that thrilling scene consists of a ridiculous conversation about food, and flirtation between a frivolous old lawyer and a fashionable girl. We can say nothing about what makes these scenes, except that the wind bloweth where it listeth, and that here the wind blows strong.

It is in this quality of what may be called spiritual adventurousness that Scott stands at so different an elevation to the whole of the contemporary crop of romancers who have followed the leadership of Dumas. There has, indeed, been a great and inspiriting revival of romance in our time, but it is partly frustrated in almost every case by this rooted conception that romance consists in the vast multiplication of incidents and the violent acceleration of narrative. The heroes of Mr. Stanley Weyman scarcely ever have their swords out of their hands; the deeper presence of romance is far better felt when the sword is at the hip ready for innumerable adventures too terrible to be pictured. The Stanley Weyman hero has scarcely time to eat his supper except in the act of leaping from a window or whilst his other hand is employed in lunging with a rapier. In Scott's heroes, on the other hand, there is no characteristic so typical or so worthy of humour as their disposition to linger over their meals. The conviviality of the Clerk of Copmanhurst or of Mr. Pleydell, and the thoroughly solid things they are described as eating, is one of the most perfect of Scott's poetic touches. In short, Mr. Stanley Weyman is filled with the conviction that the sole essence of romance is to move with insatiable rapidity from incident to incident. In the truer romance of Scott there is more of the sentiment of "Oh! still delay, thou art so fair"! more of a certain patriarchal enjoyment of things as they are—of the sword by the side and the wine-cup in the hand. Romance, indeed, does not consist by any means so much in experiencing adventures as in being ready for them. How little the actual boy cares for incidents in comparison to tools and weapons may be tested by the fact that the most popular story of adventure is concerned with a man who lived for years on a desert island with two guns and a sword, which he never had to use on an enemy.

Closely connected with this is one of the charges most commonly brought against Scott, particularly in his own day—the charge of a fanciful and monotonous insistence upon the details of armour and costume. The critic in the *Edinburgh Review* said indignantly that he could tolerate a somewhat detailed description of the apparel of Marmion, but when it came to an equally detailed account of the apparel of his pages and yeomen the mind could bear it no longer. The only thing to be said about that critic is that he had never been a little boy. He foolishly imagined that Scott valued the plume and dagger of Marmion for Marmion's sake. Not being himself romantic, he could not understand that Scott valued the plume because it was a plume, and the dagger because it was a dagger. Like a child, he loved weapons with a manual materialistic love, as one loves the softness of fur or the coolness of marble. One of the profound philosophical truths which are almost confined to infants is this love of things, not for their use or origin, but for their own inherent characteristics, the child's love of the toughness of wood, the wetness of water, the magnificent soapiness of soap. So it was with Scott, who had so much of the child in him. Human beings were perhaps the principal characters in his stories, but they were certainly not the only characters. A battle-axe was a person of importance, a castle had a character and ways of its own. A church bell had a word to say in the matter. Like a true child, he almost ignored the distinction between the animate and inanimate. A two-handed sword might be carried only by a menial in a procession, but it was something important and immeasurably fascinating—it was a two-handed sword.

There is one quality which is supreme and continuous in Scott which is little appreciated at present. One of the values we have really lost in recent fiction is the value of eloquence. The modern literary artist is compounded of almost every man except the orator. Yet Shakespeare and Scott are certainly alike in this, that they could both, if literature had failed, have earned a living as professional demagogues. The feudal heroes in the "Waverley Novels" retort upon each other with a passionate dignity, haughty and yet singularly human, which can hardly be paralleled in political eloquence except in "Julius Cæsar." With a certain fiery impartiality which stirs the blood, Scott distributes his noble orations equally among saints and villains. He may deny a villain every virtue or triumph, but he cannot endure to deny him a telling word; he will ruin a man, but he will not silence him. In truth, one of Scott's most splendid traits is his difficulty, or rather incapacity, for despising any of his characters. He did not scorn the most revolting miscreant as the realist of today commonly scorns his own hero. Though his soul may be in rags, every man of Scott can speak like a king.

This quality, as I have said, is sadly to seek in the fiction of the passing hour. The realist would, of course, repudiate the bare idea of putting a bold and brilliant tongue in every man's head, but even where the moment of the story naturally demands eloquence the eloquence seems frozen in the tap. Take any contemporary work of fiction and turn to the scene where the young Socialist denounces the millionaire, and then compare the stilted sociological lecture given by that self-sacrificing bore with the surging joy of words in Rob Roy's declaration of himself, or Athelstane's defiance of De Bracy. That ancient sea of human passion upon which high words and great phrases are the resplendent foam is just now at a low ebb. We have even gone the length of congratulating ourselves because we can see the mud and the monsters at the bottom.

In politics there is not a single man whose position is due to eloquence in the first degree; its place is taken by repartees and rejoinders purely intellectual, like those of an omnibus conductor. In discussing questions like the farm-burning in South Africa no critic of the war uses his material as Burke or Grattan (perhaps exaggeratively) would have used it—the speaker is content with facts and expositions of facts. In another age he might have risen and hurled that great song in prose, perfect as prose and yet rising into a chant, which Meg Merrilies hurled at Ellangowan, at the rulers of Britain: "Ride your ways. Laird of Ellangowan; ride your ways, Godfrey Bertram—this day have ye quenched seven smoking hearths. See if the fire in your ain parlour burns the blyther for that. Ye have riven the thack of seven cottar houses. Look if your ain roof-tree stands the faster for that. Ye may stable your stirks in the sheilings of Dern-cleugh. See that the hare does not couch on the hearthstane of Ellangowan. Ride your ways, Godfrey Bertram."

The reason is, of course, that these men are afraid of bombast and Scott was not. A man will not reach eloquence if he is afraid of bombast, just as a man will not jump a hedge if he is afraid of a ditch. As the object of all eloquence is to find the least common denominator of men's souls, to fall just within the natural comprehension, it cannot obviously have any chance with a literary ambition which aims at falling just outside it. It is quite right to invent subtle analyses and detached criticisms, but it is unreasonable to expect them to be punctuated with roars of popular applause. It is possible to conceive of a mob shouting any central and simple sentiment, good or bad, but it is impossible to think of a mob shouting a distinction in terms. In the matter of eloquence, the whole question is one of the immediate effect of greatness, such as is produced even by fine bombast. It is absurd to call it merely superficial; here there is no question of superficiality; we might as well call a stone that strikes us between the eyes merely superficial. The very word "superficial" is founded on a fundamental mistake about life, the idea that second thoughts are best. The superficial impression of the world is by far the deepest. What we really feel, naturally and casually, about the look of skies and trees and the face of friends, that and that alone will almost certainly remain our vital philosophy to our dying day.

Scott's bombast, therefore, will always be stirring to anyone who approaches it, as he should approach all literature, as a little child. We could easily excuse the contemporary critic for not admiring melodramas and adventure stories, and Punch and Judy, if he would admit that it was a slight deficiency in his artistic sensibilities. Beyond all question, it marks a lack of literary instinct to be unable to simplify one's mind at the first signal of the advance of romance. "You do me wrong," said Brian de Bois-Guilbert to Rebecca. "Many a law, many a commandment have I broken, but my word, never." "Die," cries Balfour of Burley to the villain in "Old Mortality." "Die, hoping nothing, believing nothing—" "And fearing nothing," replies the other. This is the old and honourable fine art of bragging, as it was practised by the great worthies of antiquity. The man who cannot appreciate it goes along with the man who cannot appreciate beef or claret or a game with children or a brass band. They are afraid of making fools of themselves, and are unaware that that transformation has already been triumphantly effected.

Scott is separated, then, from much of the later conception of fiction by this quality of eloquence. The whole of the best and finest work of the modern novelist (such as the work of Mr. Henry James) is primarily concerned with that delicate and fascinating speech which burrows deeper and deeper like a mole; but we have wholly forgotten that speech which mounts higher and higher like a wave and falls in a crashing peroration. Perhaps the most thoroughly brilliant and typical man of this decade is Mr. Bernard Shaw. In his admirable play of "Candida" it is clearly a part of the character of the Socialist clergyman that he should be eloquent, but he is not eloquent because the whole "G.B.S." condition of mind renders impossible that poetic simplicity which eloquence requires. Scott takes his heroes and villains seriously, which is, after all, the way that heroes and villains take themselves—especially villains. It is the custom to call these old romantic poses artificial; but the word artificial is the last and silliest evasion of criticism. There was never anything in the world that was really artificial. It had some motive or ideal behind it, and generally a much better one than we think.

Of the faults of Scott as an artist it is not very necessary to speak, for faults are generally and easily pointed out, while there is yet no adequate valuation of the varieties and contrasts of virtue. We have compiled a complete botanical classification of the weeds in the poetical garden, but the flowers still flourish, neglected and nameless. It is true, for example, that Scott had an incomparably stiff and pedantic way of dealing with his heroines: he made a lively girl of eighteen refuse an offer in the language of Dr. Johnson. To him, as to most men of his time, woman was not an individual, but an institution—a toast that was drunk some time after that of Church and King. But it is far better to consider the difference rather as a special merit, in that he stood for all those clean and bracing shocks of incident which are untouched by passion or weakness, for a certain breezy bachelorhood, which is almost essential to the literature of adventure. With all his faults, and all his triumphs, he stands for the great mass of natural manliness which must be absorbed into art unless art is to be a mere luxury and freak. An appreciation of Scott might be made almost a test of decadence. If ever we lose touch with this one most reckless and defective writer, it will be a proof to us that we have erected round ourselves a false cosmos, a world of lying and horrible perfection, leaving outside of it Walter Scott and that strange old world which is as confused and as indefensible and as inspiring and as healthy as he.

BRET HARTE

There are more than nine hundred and ninety-nine excellent reasons which we could all have for admiring the work of Bret Harte. But one supreme reason stands not in a certain general superiority to them all—a reason which may be stated in three propositions united in a common conclusion: first, that he was a genuine American; second, that he was a genuine humourist; and, third, that he was not an American humourist. Bret Harte had his own peculiar humour, but it had nothing in particular to do with American humour. American humour has its own peculiar excellence, but it has nothing in particular to do with Bret Harte. American humour is purely exaggerative; Bret Harte's humour was sympathetic and analytical.

In order fully to understand this, it is necessary to realise, genuinely and thoroughly, that there is such a thing as an international difference in humour. If we take the crudest joke in the world—the joke, let us say, of a man sitting down on his hat—we shall yet find that all the nations would differ in their way of treating it humourously, and that if American humour treated it at all, it would be in a purely American manner. For example, there was a case of an orator in the House of Commons, who, after denouncing all the public abuses he could think of, did sit down on his hat. An Irishman immediately rose, full of the whole wealth of Irish humour, and said, "Should I be in order, Sir, in congratulating the honourable gentleman on the fact that when he sat down on his hat his head was not in it?" Here is a glorious example of Irish humour—the bull not unconscious, not entirely conscious, but rather an idea so absurd that even the utterer of it can hardly realise how abysmally absurd it is. But every other nation would have treated the idea in a manner slightly different. The Frenchman's humour would have been logical: he would have said, "The orator denounces modern abuses and destroys to himself the top-hat: behold a good example!" What the Scotchman's humour would have said I am not so certain, but it would probably have dealt with the serious advisability of making such speeches on top of someone else's hat. But American humour on such a general theme would be the humour of exaggeration. The American humourist would say that the English politicians so often sat down on their hats that the noise of the House of Commons was one crackle of silk. He would say that when an important orator rose to speak in the House of Commons, long rows of hatters waited outside the House with note-books to take down orders from the participants in the debate. He would say that the whole hat trade of London was disorganised by the news that a clever remark had been made by a young M. P. on the subject of the imports of Jamaica. In short, American humour, neither unfathomably absurd like the Irish, nor transfiguringly lucid and appropriate like the French, nor sharp and sensible and full of realities of life like the Scotch, is simply the humour of imagination. It consists in piling towers on towers and mountains on mountains; of heaping a joke up to the stars and extending it to the end of the world.

With this distinctively American humour Bret Harte had little or nothing in common. The wild, sky-breaking humour of America has its fine qualities, but it must in the nature of things be deficient in two qualities, not only of supreme importance to life and letters, but of supreme importance to humour—reverence and sympathy. And these two qualities were knit into the closest texture of Bret Harte's humour. Everyone who has read and enjoyed Mark Twain as he ought to be read and enjoyed will remember a very funny and irreverent story about an organist who was asked to play appropriate music to an address upon the parable of the Prodigal Son, and who proceeded to play with great spirit, "We'll all get blind drunk, when Johnny comes marching home." The best way of distinguishing Bret Harte from the rest of American humour is to say that if Bret Harte had described that scene, it would in some subtle way have combined a sense of the absurdity of the incident with some sense of the sublimity and pathos of the theme. You would have felt that the organist's tune was funny, but not that the Prodigal Son was funny. But America is under a kind of despotism of humour. Everyone is afraid of humour: the meanest of human nightmares. Bret Harte had, to express the matter briefly but more or less essentially, the power of laughing not only at things, but also with them. America has laughed at things magnificently, with Gargantuan reverberations of laughter. But she has not even begun to learn the richer lesson of laughing with them.

The supreme proof of the fact that Bret Harte had the instinct of reverence may be found in the fact that he was a really great parodist. This may have the appearance of being a paradox, but, as in the case of many other paradoxes, it is not so important whether it is a paradox as whether it is not obviously true. Mere derision, mere contempt, never produced or could produce parody. A man who simply despises Paderewski for having long hair is not necessarily fitted to give an admirable imitation of his particular touch on the piano. If a man wishes to parody Paderewski's style of execution, he must emphatically go through one process first: he must admire it, and even reverence it. Bret Harte had a real power of imitating great authors, as in his parodies on Dumas, on Victor Hugo, on Charlotte Brontë. This means, and can only mean, that he had perceived the real beauty, the real ambition of Dumas and Victor Hugo and Charlotte Brontë. To take an example, Bret Harte has in his imitation of Hugo a passage like this:

> "M. Madeline was, if possible, better than M. Myriel. M. Myriel was an angel. M. Madeline was a good man." I do not know whether Victor Hugo ever used this antithesis; but I am certain that he would have used it and thanked his stars if he had thought of it. This is real parody, inseparable from admiration. It is the same in the parody of Dumas, which is arranged on the system of "Aramis killed three of them. Porthos three. Athos three." You cannot write that kind of thing unless you have first exulted in the arithmetical ingenuity of the plots of Dumas. It is the same in the parody of Charlotte Brontë, which opens with a dream of a storm-beaten cliff, containing jewels and pelicans. Bret Harte could not have written it unless he had really understood the triumph of the Brontës, the triumph of asserting that great mysteries lie under the surface of the most sullen life, and that the most real part of a man is in his dreams.

This kind of parody is for ever removed from the purview of ordinary American humour. Can anyone imagine Mark Twain, that admirable author, writing even a tolerable imitation of authors so intellectually individual as Hugo or Charlotte Brontë? Mark Twain would yield to the spirit of contempt which destroys parody. All those who hate authors fail to satirise them, for they always accuse them of the wrong faults. The enemies of Thackeray call him a worldling, instead of what he was, a man too ready to believe in the goodness of the unworldly. The enemies of Meredith call his gospel too subtle, instead of what it is, a gospel, if anything, too robust. And it is this vulgar misunderstanding which we find in most parody—which we find in all American parody—but which we never find in the parodies of Bret Harte.

> *"The skies they were ashen and sober,*
> *The streets they were dirty and drear,*
> *It was the dark month of October,*
> *In that most immemorial year.*
> *Like the skies, I was perfectly sober,*
> *But my thoughts they were palsied and sear,*
> *Yes, my thoughts were decidedly queer."*

This could only be written by a genuine admirer of Edgar Allan Poe, who permitted himself for a moment to see the fun of the thing. Parody might indeed be defined as the worshipper's half-holiday.

The same general characteristic of sympathy amounting to reverence marks Bret Harte's humour in his better-known class of works, the short stories. He does not make his characters absurd in order to make them contemptible: it might almost be said that he makes them absurd in order to make them dignified. For example, the greatest creation of Bret Harte, greater even than Colonel Starbottle (and how terrible it is to speak of anyone greater than Colonel Starbottle!) is that unutterable being who goes by the name of Yuba Bill. He is, of course, the coach-driver in the Bret Harte district. Some ingenious person, whose remarks I read the other day, had compared him on this ground with old Mr. Weller. It would be difficult to find a comparison indicating a more completely futile instinct for literature. Tony Weller and Yuba Bill were both coach-drivers, and this fact establishes a resemblance just about as much as the fact that Jobson in "Rob Roy" and George Warrington in "Pendennis" were both lawyers; or that Antonio and Mr. Pickwick were both merchants; or that Sir Galahad and Sir Willoughby Patten were both knights. Tony Weller is a magnificent grotesque. He is a gargoyle, and his mouth, like the mouths of so many gargoyles, is always open. He is garrulous, exuberant, flowery, preposterously sociable. He holds that great creed of the convivial, the creed which is at the back of so much that is greatest in Dickens, the creed that eternity begins at ten o'clock at night, and that nights last forever. But Yuba Bill is a figure of a widely different character. He is not convivial; it might almost be said that he is too great ever to be sociable. A circle of quiescence and solitude such as that which might ring a saint or a hermit rings this majestic and profound humourist. His jokes do not flow upon him like those of Mr. Weller, sparkling, continual, and deliberate, like the play of a fountain in a pleasure garden; they fall suddenly and capriciously, like a crash of avalanches from a great mountain. Tony Weller has the noisy humour of London, Yuba Bill has the silent humour of the earth.

One of the worst of the disadvantages of the rich and random fertility of Bret Harte is the fact that it is very difficult to trace or recover all the stories that he has written. I have not within reach at the moment the story in which the character of Yuba Bill is exhibited in its most solemn grandeur, but I remember that it concerned a ride on the San Francisco stage coach, a difficulty arising from storm and darkness, and an intelligent young man who suggested to Yuba Bill that a certain manner of driving the coach in a certain direction might minimise the dangers of the journey. A profound silence followed the intelligent young man's suggestion, and then (I quote from memory) Yuba Bill observed at last:

"Air you settin' any value on that remark?"

The young man professed not fully to comprehend him, and Yuba Bill continued reflectively:

"'Cos there's a comic paper in 'Frisco pays for them things, and I've seen worse in it."

To be rebuked thus is like being rebuked by the Pyramids or by the starry heavens. There is about Yuba Bill this air of a pugnacious calm, a stepping back to get his distance for a shattering blow, which is like that of Dr. Johnson at his best. And the effect is inexpressively increased by the background and the whole picture which Bret Harte paints so powerfully; the stormy skies, the sombre gorge, the rocking and spinning coach, and high above the feverish passengers the huge dark form of Yuba Bill, a silent mountain of humour.

Another unrecovered and possibly irrecoverable fragment about Yuba Bill, I recall in a story about his visiting a lad who had once been his protége in the Wild West, and who had since become a distinguished literary man in Boston. Yuba Bill visits him, and on finding him in evening dress lifts up his voice in a superb lamentation over the tragedy of finding his old friend at last "a 'otel waiter." Then, vindictively pursuing the satire, he calls fiercely to his young friend, "Hi, Alphonse! bring me a patty de foy gras, damme." These are the things that make us love the eminent Bill. He is one of those who achieve the noblest and most difficult of all the triumphs of a fictitious character—the triumph of giving us the impression of having a great deal more in him than appears between the two boards of the story. Smaller characters give us the impression that the author has told the whole truth about them, greater characters give the impression that the author has given of them, not the truth, but merely a few hints and samples. In some mysterious way we seem to feel that even if Shakespeare was wrong about Falstaff, Falstaff existed and was real; that even if Dickens was wrong about Micawber, Micawber existed and was real. So we feel that there is in the great salt-sea of Yuba Bill's humour as good fish as ever came out of it. The fleeting jests which Yuba Bill throws to the coach passengers only give us the opportunity of fancying and deducing the vast mass of jests which Yuba Bill shares with his creator.

Bret Harte had to deal with countries and communities of an almost unexampled laxity, a laxity passing the laxity of savages, the laxity of civilised men grown savage. He dealt with a life which we in a venerable and historic society may find it somewhat difficult to realise. It was the life of an entirely new people, a people who, having no certain past, could have no certain future. The strangest of all the sardonic jests that history has ever played may be found in this fact: that there is a city which is of all cities the most typical of innovation and dissipation, and a certain almost splendid vulgarity, and that this city bears the name in a quaint old European language of the most perfect exponent of the simplicity and holiness of the Christian tradition; the city is called San Francisco. San Francisco, the capital of the Bret Harte country, is a city typifying novelty in a manner in which it is typified by few modern localities. San Francisco has in all probability its cathedrals, but it may well be that its cathedrals are less old and less traditional than many of our hotels. If its inhabitants built a temple to the most primal and forgotten god of whose worship we can find a trace, that temple would still be a modern thing compared with many taverns in Suffolk round which there lingers a faint tradition of Mr. Pickwick. And everything in that new gold country was new, even to the individual inhabitants. Good, bad, and indifferent, heroes and dastards, they were all men from nowhere.

Most of us have come across the practical problem of London landladies, the problem of the doubtful foreign gentleman in a street of respectable English people. Those who have done so can form some idea of what it would be to live in a street full of doubtful foreign gentlemen, in a parish, in a city, in a nation composed entirely of doubtful foreign gentlemen. Old California, at the time of the first rush after gold, was actually this paradox of the nation of foreigners. It was a republic of incognitos: no one knew who anyone else was, and only the more ill-mannered and uneasy even desired to know. In such a country as this, gentlemen took more trouble to conceal their gentility than thieves living in South Kensington would take to conceal their blackguardism. In such a country everyone is an equal, because everyone is a stranger. In such a country it is not strange if men in moral matters feel something of the irresponsibility of a dream. To plan plans which are continually miscarrying against men who are continually disappearing by the assistance of you know not whom, to crush you know not whom, this must be a demoralising life for any man; it must be beyond description demoralising for those who have been trained in no lofty or orderly scheme of right. Small blame to them indeed if they become callous and supercilious and cynical. And the great glory and achievement of Bret Harte consists in this, that he realised that they do not become callous, supercilious, and cynical, but that they do become sentimental and romantic, and profoundly affectionate. He discovered the intense sensibility of the primitive man. To him we owe the realisation of the fact that while modern barbarians of genius like Mr. Henley, and in his weaker moments Mr. Rudyard Kipling, delight in describing the coarseness and crude cynicism and fierce humour of the unlettered classes, the unlettered classes are in reality highly sentimental and religious, and not in the least like the creations of Mr. Henley and Mr. Kipling. Bret Harte tells the truth about the wildest, the grossest, the most rapacious of all the districts of the earth—the truth that, while it is very rare indeed in the world to find a thoroughly good man, it is rarer still, rare to the point of monstrosity, to find a man who does not either desire to be one, or imagine that he is one already.

ALFRED THE GREAT

The celebrations in connection with the millenary of King Alfred struck a note of sympathy in the midst of much that was unsympathetic, because, altogether apart from any peculiar historical opinions, all men feel the sanctifying character of that which is at once strong and remote; the ancient thing is always the most homely, and the distant thing the most near. The only possible peacemaker is a dead man, ever since by the sublime religious story a dead man only could reconcile heaven and earth. In a certain sense we always feel the past ages as human, and our own age as strangely and even weirdly dehumanised. In our own time the details overpower us; men's badges and buttons seem to grow larger and larger as in a horrible dream. To study humanity in the present is like studying a mountain with a magnifying glass; to study it in the past is like studying it through a telescope.

For this reason England, like every other great and historic nation, has sought its typical hero in remote and ill-recorded times. The personal and moral greatness of Alfred is, indeed, beyond question. It does not depend any more than the greatness of any other human hero upon the accuracy of any or all of the stories that are told about him. Alfred may not have done one of the things which are reported of him, but it is immeasurably easier to do every one of those things than to be the man of whom such things are reported falsely. Fable is, generally speaking, far more accurate than fact, for fable describes a man as he was to his own age, fact describes him as he is to a handful of inconsiderable antiquarians many centuries after. Whether Alfred watched the cakes for the neat-herd's wife, whether he sang songs in the Danish camp, is of no interest to anyone except those who set out to prove under considerable disadvantages that they are genealogically descended from him. But the man is better pictured in these stories than in any number of modern realistic trivialities about his favourite breakfast and his favourite musical composer. Fable is more historical than fact, because fact tells us about one man and fable tells us about a million men. If we read of a man who could make green grass red and turn the sun into the moon, we may not believe these particular details about him, but we learn something infinitely more important than such trivialities, the fact that men could look into his face and believe it possible. The glory and greatness of Alfred, therefore, is like that of all the heroes of the morning of the world, set far beyond the chance of that strange and sudden dethronement which may arise from the unsealing of a manuscript or the turning over of a stone. Men may have told lies when they said that he first entrapped the Danes with his song and then overcame them with his armies, but we know very well that it is not of us that such lies are told. There may be myths clustering about each of our personalities; local saga-men and chroniclers have very likely circulated the story that we are addicted to drink, or that we ferociously ill-use our wives. But they do not commonly lie to the effect that we have shed our blood to save all the inhabitants of the street. A story grows easily, but a heroic story is not a very easy thing to evoke. Wherever that exists we may be pretty certain that we are in the presence of a dark but powerful historic personality. We are in the presence of a thousand lies all pointing with their fantastic fingers to one undiscovered truth.

Upon this ground alone every encouragement is due to the cult of Alfred. Every nation requires to have behind it some historic personality, the validity of which is proved, as the validity of a gun is proved, by its long range. It is wonderful and splendid that we treasure, not the truth, but the very gossip about a man who died a thousand years ago. We may say to him, as M. Rostand says to the Austrian Prince:

> "Dors, ce n'est pas toujours la Légende qui ment:
> Une rêve est parfois moins trompeur qu'un document."

To have a man so simple and so honourable to represent us in the darkness of primeval history, binds all the intervening centuries together, and mollifies all their monstrosities. It makes all history more comforting and intelligible; it makes the desolate temple of the ages as human as an inn parlour.

But whether it come through reliable facts or through more reliable falsehoods the personality of Alfred has its own unmistakable colour and stature. Lord Rosebery uttered a profound truth when he said that that personality was peculiarly English. The great magnificence of the English character is expressed in the word "service." There is, perhaps, no nation so vitally theocratical as the English; no nation in which the strong men have so consistently preferred the instrumental to the despotic attitude, the pleasures of the loyal to the pleasures of the royal position. We have had tyrants like Edward I. and Queen Elizabeth, but even our tyrants have had the worried and responsible air of stewards of a great estate. Our typical hero is such a man as the Duke of Wellington, who had every kind of traditional and external arrogance, but at the back of all that the strange humility which made it physically possible for him without a gleam of humour or discomfort to go on his knees to a preposterous bounder like George IV. Across the infinite wastes of time and through all the mists of legend we still feel the presence in Alfred of this strange and unconscious self-effacement. After the fullest estimate of our misdeeds we can still say that our very despots have been less self-assertive than many popular patriots. As we consider these things we grow more and more impatient of any modern tendencies towards the enthronement of a more self-conscious and theatrical ideal. Lord Rosebery called up before our imaginations the picture of what Alfred would have thought of the vast modern developments of his nation, its immense fleet, its widespread Empire, its enormous contribution to the mechanical civilisation of the world. It cannot be anything but profitable to conceive Alfred as full of astonishment and admiration at these things; it cannot be anything but good for us that we should realise that to the child-like eyes of a great man of old time our inventions and appliances have not the vulgarity and ugliness that we see in them. To Alfred a steamboat would be a new and sensational sea-dragon, and the penny postage a miracle achieved by the despotism of a demi-god.

But when we have realised all this there is something more to be said in connection with Lord Rosebery's vision. What would King Alfred have said if he had been asked to expend the money which he devoted to the health and education of his people upon a struggle with some race of Visigoths or Parthians inhabiting a small section of a distant continent? What would he have said if he had known that that science of letters which he taught to England would eventually be used not to spread truth, but to drug the people with political assurances as imbecile in themselves as the assurance that fire does not burn and water does not drown?

What would he have said if the same people who, in obedience to that ideal of service and sanity of which he was the example, had borne every privation in order to defeat Napoleon, should come at last to find no better compliment to one of their heroes than to call him the Napoleon of South Africa? What would he have said if that nation for which he had inaugurated a long line of incomparable men of principle should forget all its traditions and coquette with the immoral mysticism of the man of destiny?

Let us follow these things by all means if we find them good, and can see nothing better. But to pretend that Alfred would have admired them is like pretending that St. Dominic would have seen eye to eye with Mr. Bradlaugh, or that Fra Angelico would have revelled in the posters of Mr. Aubrey Beardsley. Let us follow them if we will, but let us take honestly all the disadvantages of our change; in the wildest moment of triumph let us feel the shadow upon our glories of the shame of the great king.

MAETERLINCK

The selection of "Thoughts from Maeterlinck" is a very creditable and also a very useful compilation. Many modern critics object to the hacking and hewing of a consistent writer which is necessary for this kind of work, but upon more serious consideration, the view is not altogether adequate. Maeterlinck is a very great man; and in the long run this process of mutilation has happened to all great men. It was the mark of a great patriot to be drawn and quartered and his head set on one spike in one city and his left leg on another spike in another city. It was the mark of a saint that even these fragments began to work miracles. So it has been with all the very great men of the world. However careless, however botchy, may be the version of Maeterlinck or of anyone else given in such a selection as this, it is assuredly far less careless and far less botchy than the version, the parody, the wild misrepresentation of Maeterlinck which future ages will hear and distant critics be called upon to consider.

No one can feel any reasonable doubt that we have heard about Christ and Socrates and Buddha and St. Francis a mere chaos of excerpts, a mere book of quotations. But from those fragmentary epigrams we can deduce greatness as clearly as we can deduce Venus from the torso of Venus or Hercules *ex pede Herculem*. If we knew nothing else about the Founder of Christianity, for example, beyond the fact that a religious teacher lived in a remote country, and in the course of his peregrinations and proclamations consistently called Himself "the Son of Man," we should know by that alone that he was a man of almost immeasurable greatness. If future ages happened to record nothing else about Socrates except that he owned his title to be the wisest of men because he knew that he knew nothing, they would be able to deduce from that the height and energy of his civilisation, the glory that was Greece. The credit of such random compilations as that which "E.S.S." and Mr. George Allen have just effected is quite secure. It is the pure, pedantic, literal editions, the complete works of this author or that author which are forgotten. It is such books as this that have revolutionised the destiny of the world. Great things like Christianity or Platonism have never been founded upon consistent editions; all of them have been founded upon scrap-books.

The position of Maeterlinck in modern life is a thing too obvious to be easily determined in words. It is, perhaps, best expressed by saying that it is the great glorification of the inside of things at the expense of the outside. There is one great evil in modern life for which nobody has found even approximately a tolerable description: I can only invent a word and call it "remotism." It is the tendency to think first of things which, as a matter of fact, lie far away from the actual centre of human experience. Thus people say, "All our knowledge of life begins with the amoeba." It is false; our knowledge of life begins with ourselves. Thus they say that the British Empire is glorious, and at the very word Empire they think at once of Australia and New Zealand, and Canada, and Polar bears, and parrots and kangaroos, and it never occurs to any one of them to think of the Surrey Hills. The one real struggle in modern life is the struggle between the man like Maeterlinck, who sees the inside as the truth, and the man like Zola, who sees the outside as the truth. A hundred cases might be given. We may take, for the sake of argument, the case of what is called falling in love. The sincere realist, the man who believes in a certain finality in physical science, says, "You may, if you like, describe this thing as a divine and sacred and incredible vision; that is your sentimental theory about it. But what it is, is an animal and sexual instinct designed for certain natural purposes." The man on the other side, the idealist, replies, with quite equal confidence, that this is the very reverse of the truth. I put it as it has always struck me; he replies, "Not at all. You may, if you like, describe this thing as an animal and sexual instinct, designed for certain natural purposes; that is your philosophical or zoölogical theory about it. What it is, beyond all doubt of any kind, is a divine and sacred and incredible vision." The fact that it is an animal necessity only comes to the naturalistic philosopher after looking abroad, studying its origins and results, constructing an explanation of its existence, more or less natural and conclusive. The fact that it is a spiritual triumph comes to the first errand boy who happens to feel it. If a lad of seventeen falls in love and is struck dead by a hansom cab an hour afterwards, he has known the thing as it is, a spiritual ecstasy; he has never come to trouble about the thing as it may be, a physical destiny. If anyone says that falling in love is an animal thing, the answer is very simple. The only way of testing the matter is to ask those who are experiencing it, and none of those would admit for a moment that it was an animal thing.

Maeterlinck's appearance in Europe means primarily this subjective intensity; by this the materialism is not overthrown: materialism is undermined. He brings, not something which is more poetic than realism, not something which is more spiritual than realism, not something which is more right than realism, but something which is more real than realism. He discovers the one indestructible thing. This material world on which such vast systems have been superimposed—this may mean anything. It may be a dream, it may be a joke, it may be a trap or temptation, it may be a charade, it may be the beatific vision: the only thing of which we are certain is this human soul. This human soul finds itself alone in a terrible world, afraid of the grass. It has brought forth poetry and religion in order to explain matters; it will bring them forth again. It matters not one atom how often the lulls of materialism and scepticism occur; they are always broken by the reappearance of a fanatic. They have come in our time: they have been broken by Maeterlinck.

RUSKIN[2]

I do not think anyone could find any fault with the way in which Mr. Collingwood has discharged his task, except, of course, Mr. Ruskin himself, who would certainly have scored through all the eulogies in passionate red ink and declared that his dear friend had selected for admiration the very parts of his work which were vile, brainless, and revolting. That, however, was merely Ruskin's humour, and one of the deepest disappointments with Mr. Collingwood is that he, like everyone else, fails to appreciate Ruskin as a humourist. Yet he was a great humourist: half the explosions which are solemnly scolded as "one-sided" were simply meant to be one-sided, were mere laughing experiments in language. Like a woman, he saw the humour of his own prejudices, did not sophisticate them by logic, but deliberately exaggerated them by rhetoric. One tenth of his paradoxes would have made the fortune of a modern young man with gloves of an art yellow. He was as fond of nonsense as Mr. Max Beerbohm. Only ... he was fond of other things too. He did not ask humanity to dine on pickles.

But while his kaleidoscope of fancy and epigram gives him some kinship with the present day, he was essentially of an earlier type: he was the last of the prophets. With him vanishes the secret of that early Victorian simplicity which gave a man the courage to mount a pulpit above the head of his fellows. Many elements, good and bad, have destroyed it; humility as well as fear, camaraderie as well as scepticism, have bred in us a desire to give our advice lightly and persuasively, to mask our morality, to whisper a word and glide away. The contrast was in some degree typified in the House of Commons under the last leadership of Mr. Gladstone: the old order with its fist on the box, and the new order

2   "The Life of John Ruskin." By W.G. Collingwood. London: Methuen.

with its feet on the table. Doubtless the wine of that prophecy was too strong even for the strong heads that carried it. It made Ruskin capricious and despotic, Tennyson lonely and whimsical, Carlyle harsh to the point of hatred, and Kingsley often rabid to the ruin of logic and charity. One alone of that race of giants, the greatest and most neglected, was sober after the cup. No mission, no frustration could touch with hysteria the humanity of Robert Browning.

But though Ruskin seems to close the roll of the militant prophets, we feel how needful are such figures when we consider with what pathetic eagerness men pay prophetic honours even to those who disclaim the prophetic character. Ibsen declares that he only depicts life, that as far as he is concerned there is nothing to be done, and still armies of "Ibsenites" rally to the flag and enthusiastically do nothing. I have found traces of a school which avowedly follows Mr. Henry James: an idea full of humour. I like to think of a crowd with pikes and torches shouting passages from "The Awkward Age." It is right and proper for a multitude to declare its readiness to follow a prophet to the end of the world, but if he himself explains, with pathetic gesticulations, that he is only going for a walk in the park, there is not much for the multitude to do. But the disciple of Ruskin had plenty to do. He made roads; in his spare moments he studied the whole of geology and botany. He lifted up paving stones and got down into early Florentine cellars, where, by hanging upside down, he could catch a glimpse of a Cimabue unpraisable but by divine silence. He rushed from one end of a city to the other comparing ceilings. His limbs were weary, his clothes were torn, and in his eyes was that unfathomable joy of life which man will never know again until once more he takes himself seriously.

Mr. Collingwood's excellent chapters on the art criticism of Ruskin would be better, in my opinion, if they showed more consciousness of the after revolutions that have reversed, at least in detail, much of Ruskin's teaching. We no longer think that art became valueless when it was first corrupted with anatomical accuracy. But if we return to that Raphaelism to which he was so unjust, let us not fall into the old error of intelligent reactionaries, that of ignoring our own debt to revolutions. Ruskin could not destroy the market of Raphaelism, but he could and did destroy its monopoly. We may go back to the Renaissance, but let us remember that we go back free. We can picnic now in the ruins of our dungeon and deride our deliverer.

But neither in Mr. Collingwood's book nor in Ruskin's own delightful "Præterita" shall we ever get to the heart of the matter. The work of Ruskin and his peers remains incomprehensible by the very completeness of their victory. Fallen forever is that vast brick temple of Utilitarianism, of which we may find the fragments but never renew the spell. Liberal Unionists howl in its high places, and in its ruins Mr. Lecky builds his nest. Its records read with something of the mysterious arrogance of Chinese: hardly a generation away from us, we read of a race who believed in the present with the same sort of servile optimism with which the Oriental believes in the past. It may be that banging his head against that roof for twenty years did not improve the temper of the prophet. But he made what he praised in the old Italian pictures—"an opening into eternity."

QUEEN VICTORIA

Anyone who possesses spiritual or political courage has made up his mind to a prospect of immutable mutability; but even in a "transformation" there is something catastrophic in the removal of the back scene. It is a truism to say of the wise and noble lady who is gone from us that we shall always remember her; but there is a subtler and higher compliment still in confessing that we often forgot her. We forgot her as we forget the sunshine, as we forget the postulates of an argument, as we commonly forget our own existence. Mr. Gladstone is the only figure whose loss prepared us for such earthquakes altering the landscape. But Mr. Gladstone seemed a fixed and stationary object in our age for the same reason that one railway train looks stationary from another; because he and the age of progress were both travelling at the same impetuous rate of speed. In the end, indeed, it was probably the age that dropped behind. For a symbol of the Queen's position we must rather recur to the image of a stretch of scenery, in which she was as a mountain so huge and familiar that its disappearance would make the landscape round our own door seem like a land of strangers. She had an inspired genius for the familiarising virtues; her sympathy and sanity made us feel at home even in an age of revolutions. That indestructible sense of security which for good and evil is so typical of our nation, that almost scornful optimism which, in the matter of ourselves, cannot take peril or even decadence seriously, reached by far its highest and healthiest form in the sense that we were watched over by one so thoroughly English in her silence and self-control, in her shrewd trustfulness and her brilliant inaction. Over and above those sublime laws of labour and pity by which she ordered her life, there are a very large number of minor intellectual matters in which we might learn a lesson from the Queen. There is one especially which is increasingly needed in an age when moral claims become complicated and hysterical. That Queen Victoria was a model of political unselfishness is well known; it is less often remarked that few modern people have an unselfishness so completely free from morbidity, so fully capable of deciding a moral question without exaggerating its importance. No eminent person of our time has been so utterly devoid of that disease of self-assertion which is often rampant among the unselfish. She had one most rare and valuable faculty, the faculty of letting things pass—Acts of Parliament and other things. Her predecessors, whether honest men or knaves, were attacked every now and then with a nightmare of despotic responsibility; they suddenly conceived that it rested with them to save the world and the Protestant Constitution. Queen Victoria had far too much faith in the world to try to save it. She knew that Acts of Parliament, even bad Acts of Parliament, do not destroy nations. But she knew that ignorance, ill-temper, tyranny, and officiousness do destroy nations, and not upon any provocation would she set an example in these things. We fancy that this sense of proportion, this largeness and coolness of intellectual magnanimity is the one of the thousand virtues of Queen Victoria of which the near future will stand most in need. We are gaining many new mental powers, and with them new mental responsibilities. In psychology, in sociology, above all in education, we are learning to do a great many clever things. Unless we are much mistaken the next great task will be to learn not to do them. If that time comes, assuredly we cannot do better than turn once more to the memory of the great Queen who for seventy years followed through every possible tangle and distraction the fairy thread of common sense.

We are suffering just now from an outbreak of the imagination which exhibits itself in politics and the most unlikely places. The German Emperor, for example, is neither a tyrant nor a lunatic, as used to be absurdly represented; he is simply a minor poet; and he feels just as any minor poet would feel if he found himself on the throne of Barbarossa. The revival of militarism and ecclesiasticism is an invasion of politics by the artistic sense; it is heraldry rather than chivalry that is lusted after. Amid all this waving of wands and flaunting of uniforms, all this hedonistic desire to make the most of everything, there is something altogether quiet and splendid about the sober disdain with which this simple and courteous lady in a black dress left idle beside her the sceptre of a hundred tyrants. The heart of the whole nation warmed as it had never warmed for centuries at the thought of having in their midst a woman who cared nothing for her rights, and nothing for those fantastic duties which are more egotistical than rights themselves.

The work of the Queen for progressive politics has surely been greatly underrated. She invented democratic monarchy as much as James Watt invented the steam engine. William IV., from whom we think of her as inheriting her Constitutional position, held in fact a position entirely different to that which she now hands on to Edward VII. William IV. was a limited monarch; that is to say, he had a definite, open, and admitted power in politics, but it was a limited power. Queen Victoria was not a limited monarch; in the only way in which she cared to be a monarch at all she was as unlimited as Haroun Alraschid. She had unlimited willing obedience, and unlimited social supremacy. To her belongs the credit of inventing a new kind of monarchy; in which the Crown, by relinquishing the whole of that political and legal department of life which is concerned with coercion, regimentation, and punishment, was enabled to rise above it and become the symbol of the sweeter and purer relations of humanity, the social intercourse which leads and does not drive. Too much cannot be said for the wise audacity and confident completeness with which the Queen cut away all those cords of political supremacy to which her predecessors had clung madly as the only stays of the monarchy. She had her reward. For while William IV.'s supremacy may be called a survival, it is not too much to say that the Queen's supremacy might be called a prophecy. By lifting a figure purely human over the heads of judges and warriors, we uttered in some symbolic fashion the abiding, if unreasoning, hope which dwells in all human hearts, that some day we may find a simpler solution of the woes of nations than the summons and the treadmill, that we may find in some such influence as the social influence of a woman, what was called in the noble old language of mediæval monarchy, "a fountain of mercy and a fountain of honour."

In the universal reverence paid to the Queen there was hardly anywhere a touch of snobbishness. Snobbishness, in so far as it went out towards former sovereigns, went out to them as aristocrats rather than as kings, as heads of that higher order of men, who were almost angels or demons in their admitted superiority to common lines of conduct. This kind of reverence was always a curse: nothing can be conceived as worse for the mass of the people than that they should think the morality for which they have to struggle an inferior morality, a thing unfitted for a haughtier class. But of this patrician element there was hardly a trace in the dignity of the Queen. Indeed, the degree to which the middle and lower classes took her troubles and problems to their hearts was almost grotesque in its familiarity. No one thought of the Queen as an aristocrat like the Duke of Devonshire, or even as a member of the governing classes like Mr. Chamberlain. Men thought of her as something nearer to them even in being further off; as one who was a good queen, and who would have been, had her fate demanded, with equal cheerfulness, a good washer-woman. Herein lay her unexampled triumph, the greatest and perhaps the last triumph of monarchy. Monarchy in its healthiest days had the same basis as democracy: the belief in human nature when entrusted with power. A king was only the first citizen who received the franchise.

Both royalty and religion have been accused of despising humanity, and in practice it has been too often true; but after all both the conception of the prophet and that of the king were formed by paying humanity the supreme compliment of selecting from it almost at random. This daring idea that a healthy human being, when thrilled by all the trumpets of a great trust, would rise to the situation, has often been tested, but never with such complete success as in the case of our dead Queen. On her was piled the crushing load of a vast and mystical tradition, and she stood up straight under it. Heralds proclaimed her as the anointed of God, and it did not seem presumptuous. Brave men died in thousands shouting her name, and it did not seem unnatural. No mere intellect, no mere worldly success could, in this age of bold inquiry, have sustained that tremendous claim; long ago we should have stricken Cæsar and dethroned Napoleon. But these glories and these sacrifices did not seem too much to celebrate a hardworking human nature; they were possible because at the heart of our Empire was nothing but a defiant humility. If the Queen had stood for any novel or fantastic imperial claims, the whole would have seemed a nightmare; the whole was successful because she stood, and no one could deny that she stood, for the humblest, the shortest and the most indestructible of human gospels, that when all troubles and troublemongers have had their say, our work can be done till sunset, our life can be lived till death.

THE GERMAN EMPEROR

The list of the really serious, the really convinced, the really important and comprehensible people now alive includes, as most Englishmen would now be prepared to admit, the German Emperor. He is a practical man and a poet. I do not know whether there are still people in existence who think there is some kind of faint antithesis between these two characters; but I incline to think there must be, because of the surprise which the career of the German Emperor has generally evoked. When he came to the throne it became at once apparent that he was poetical; people assumed in consequence that he was unpractical; that he would plunge Europe into war, that he would try to annex France, that he would say he was the Emperor of Russia, that he would stand on his head in the Reichstag, that he would become a pirate on the Spanish Main. Years upon years have passed; he has gone on making speeches, he has gone on talking about God and his sword, he has poured out an ever increased rhetoric and æstheticism. And yet all the time people have slowly and surely realised that he knows what he is about, that he is one of the best friends of peace, that his influence on Europe is not only successful, but in many ways good, that he knows what world he is living in better than a score of materialists.

The explanation never comes to them—he is a poet; therefore, a practical man. The affinity of the two words, merely as words, is much nearer than many people suppose, for the matter of that. There is one Greek word for "I do" from which we get the word practical, and another Greek word for "I do" from which we get the word poet. I was doubtless once informed of a profound difference between the two, but I have forgotten it. The two words practical and poetical may mean two subtly different things in that old and subtle language, but they mean the same in English and the same in the long run. It is ridiculous to suppose that the man who can understand the inmost intricacies of a human being who has never existed at all cannot make a guess at the conduct of man who lives next door. It is idle to say that a man who has himself felt the mad longing under the mad moon for a vagabond life cannot know why his son runs away to sea. It is idle to say that a man who has himself felt the hunger for any kind of exhilaration, from angel or devil, cannot know why his butler takes to drink. It is idle to say that a man who has been fascinated with the wild fastidiousness of destiny does not know why stockbrokers gamble, to say that a man who has been knocked into the middle of eternal life by a face in a crowd does not know why the poor marry young; that a man who found his path to all things kindly and pleasant blackened and barred suddenly by the body of a man does not know what it is to desire murder. It is idle, in short, for a man who has created men to say that he does not understand them. A man who is a poet may, of course, easily make mistakes in these personal and practical relations; such mistakes and similar ones have been made by poets; such mistakes and greater ones have been made by soldiers and statesmen and men of business. But in so far as a poet is in these things less of a practical man he is also less of a poet.

If Shakespeare really married a bad wife when he had conceived the character of Beatrice he ought to have been ashamed of himself: he had failed not only in his life, he had failed in his art. If Balzac got into rows with his publishers he ought to be rebuked and not commiserated, having evolved so many consistent business men from his own inside. The German Emperor is a poet, and therefore he succeeds, because poetry is so much nearer to reality than all the other human occupations. He is a poet, and succeeds because the majority of men are poets. It is true, if that matter is at all important, that the German Emperor is not a good poet. The majority of men are poets, only they happen to be bad poets. The German Emperor fails ridiculously, if that is all that is in question, in almost every one of the artistic occupations to which he addresses himself: he is neither a first-rate critic, nor a first-rate musician, nor a first-rate painter, nor a first-rate poet. He is a twelfth-rate poet, but because he is a poet at all he knocks to pieces all the first-rate politicians in the war of politics.

Having made clear my position so far, I discover with a certain amount of interest that I have not yet got to the subject of these remarks. The German Emperor is a poet, and although, as far as I know, every line he ever wrote may be nonsense, he is a poet in this real sense, that he has realised the meaning of every function he has performed. Why should we jeer at him because he has a great many uniforms, for instance? The very essence of the really imaginative man is that he realises the various types or capacities in which he can appear. Every one of us, or almost every one of us, does in reality fulfil almost as many offices as Pooh-Bah. Almost every one of us is a ratepayer, an immortal soul, an Englishman, a baptised person, a mammal, a minor poet, a juryman, a married man, a bicyclist, a Christian, a purchaser of newspapers, and a critic of Mr. Alfred Austin. We ought to have uniforms for all these things. How beautiful it would be if we appeared to-morrow in the uniform of a ratepayer, in brown and green, with buttons made in the shape of coins, and a blue income-tax paper tastefully arranged as a favour; or, again, if we appeared dressed as immortal souls, in a blue uniform with stars. It would be very exciting to dress up as Englishmen, or to go to a fancy dress ball as Christians.

Some of the costumes I have suggested might appear a little more difficult to carry out. The dress of a person who purchases newspapers (though it mostly consists of coloured evening editions arranged in a stiff skirt, like that of a saltatrice, round the waist of the wearer) has many mysterious points. The attire of a person prepared to criticise the Poet Laureate is something so awful and striking that I dare not even begin to describe it; the one fact which I am willing to reveal, and to state seriously and responsibly, is that it buttons up behind.

But most assuredly we ought not to abuse the Kaiser because he is fond of putting on all his uniforms; he does so because he has a large number of established and involuntary incarnations. He tries to do his duty in that state of life to which it shall please God to call him; and it so happens that he has been called to as many different estates as there are regiments in the German Army. He is a huntsman and proud of being a huntsman, an engineer and proud of being an engineer, an infantry soldier and proud of being so, a light horseman and proud of being so. There is nothing wrong in all this; the only wrong thing is that it should be confined to the merely destructive arts of war. The sight of the German Kaiser in the most magnificent of the uniforms in which he had led armies to victory is not in itself so splendid or delightful as that of many other sights which might come before us without a whisper of the alarms of war. It is not so splendid or delightful as the sight of an ordinary householder showing himself in that magnificent uniform of purple and silver which should signalise the father of three children. It is not so splendid or delightful as the appearance of a young clerk in an insurance office decorated with those three long crimson plumes which are the well-known insignia of a gentleman who is just engaged to be married. Nor can it compare with the look of a man wearing the magnificent green and silver armour by which we know one who has induced an acquaintance to give up getting drunk, or the blue and gold which is only accorded to persons who have prevented fights in the street. We belong to quite as many regiments as the German Kaiser. Our regiments are regiments that are embattled everywhere; they fight an unending fight against all that is hopeless and rapacious and of evil report. The only difference is that we have the regiments, but not the uniforms.

Only one obvious point occurs to me to add. If the Kaiser has more than any other man the sense of the poetry of the ancient things, the sword, the crown, the ship, the nation, he has the sense of the poetry of modern things also. He has one sense, and it is even a joke against him. He feels the poetry of one thing that is more poetic than sword or crown or ship or nation, the poetry of the telegram. No one ever sent a telegram who did not feel like a god. He is a god, for he is a minor poet; a minor poet, but a poet still.

TENNYSON

Mr. Morton Luce has written a short study of Tennyson which has considerable cultivation and suggestiveness, which will be sufficient to serve as a notebook for Tennyson's admirers, but scarcely sufficient, perhaps, to serve as a pamphlet against his opponents. If a critic has, as he ought to have, any of the functions anciently attributed to a prophet, it ought not to be difficult for him to prophesy that Tennyson will pass through a period of facile condemnation and neglect before we arrive at the true appreciation of his work. The same thing has happened to the most vigorous of essayists, Macaulay, and the most vigorous of romancers, Dickens, because we live in a time when mere vigour is considered a vulgar thing. The same idle and frigid reaction will almost certainly discredit the stateliness and care of Tennyson, as it has discredited the recklessness and inventiveness of Dickens. It is only necessary to remember that no action can be discredited by a reaction.

The attempts which have been made to discredit the poetical position of Tennyson are in the main dictated by an entire misunderstanding of the nature of poetry. When critics like Matthew Arnold, for example, suggest that his poetry is deficient in elaborate thought, they only prove, as Matthew Arnold proved, that they themselves could never be great poets. It is no valid accusation against a poet that the sentiment he expresses is commonplace. Poetry is always commonplace; it is vulgar in the noblest sense of that noble word. Unless a man can make the same kind of ringing appeal to absolute and admitted sentiments that is made by a popular orator, he has lost touch with emotional literature. Unless he is to some extent a demagogue, he cannot be a poet. A man who expresses in poetry new and strange and undiscovered emotions is not a poet; he is a brain specialist. Tennyson can never be discredited before any serious tribunal of criticism because the sentiments and thoughts to which he dedicates himself are those sentiments and thoughts which occur to anyone. These are the peculiar province of poetry; poetry, like religion, is always a democratic thing, even if it pretends the contrary. The faults of Tennyson, so far as they existed, were not half so much in the common character of his sentiments as in the arrogant perfection of his workmanship. He was not by any means so wrong in his faults as he was in his perfections.

Men are very much too ready to speak of men's work being ordinary, when we consider that, properly considered, every man is extraordinary. The average man is a tribal fable, like the Man-Wolf or the Wise Man of the Stoics. In every man's heart there is a revolution; how much more in every poet's? The supreme business of criticism is to discover that part of a man's work which is his and to ignore that part which belongs to others. Why should any critic of poetry spend time and attention on that part of a man's work which is unpoetical? Why should any man be interested in aspects which are uninteresting? The business of a critic is to discover the importance of men and not their crimes. It is true that the Greek word critic carries with it the meaning of a judge, and up to this point of history judges have had to do with the valuation of men's sins, and not with the valuation of their virtues.

Tennyson's work, disencumbered of all that uninteresting accretion which he had inherited or copied, resolves itself, like that of any other man of genius, into those things which he really inaugurated. Underneath all his exterior of polished and polite rectitude there was in him a genuine fire of novelty; only that, like all the able men of his period, he disguised revolution under the name of evolution. He is only a very shallow critic who cannot see an eternal rebel in the heart of the Conservative.

Tennyson had certain absolutely personal ideas, as much his own as the ideas of Browning or Meredith, though they were fewer in number. One of these, for example, was the fact that he was the first of all poets (and perhaps the last) to attempt to treat poetically that vast and monstrous vision of fact which science had recently revealed to mankind. Scientific discoveries seem commonly fables as fantastic in the ears of poets as poems in the ears of men of science. The poet is always a Ptolemaist; for him the sun still rises and the earth stands still. Tennyson really worked the essence of modern science into his poetical constitution, so that its appalling birds and frightful flowers were really part of his literary imagery. To him blind and brutal monsters, the products of the wild babyhood of the Universe, were as the daisies and the nightingales were to Keats; he absolutely realised the great literary paradox mentioned in the Book of Job: "He saw Behemoth, and he played with him as with a bird."

Instances of this would not be difficult to find. But the tests of poetry are those instances in which this outrageous scientific phraseology becomes natural and unconscious. Tennyson wrote one of his own exquisite lyrics describing the exultation of a lover on the evening before his bridal day. This would be an occasion, if ever there was one, for falling back on those ancient and assured falsehoods of the domed heaven and the flat earth in which generations of poets have made us feel at home. We can imagine the poet in such a lyric saluting the setting sun and prophesying the sun's resurrection. There is something extraordinarily typical of Tennyson's scientific faith in the fact that this, one of the most sentimental and elemental of his poems, opens with the two lines:

"Move eastward, happy earth, and leave
Yon orange sunset waning slow."

Rivers had often been commanded to flow by poets, and flowers to blossom in their season, and both were doubtless grateful for the permission. But the terrestrial globe of science has only twice, so far as we know, been encouraged in poetry to continue its course, one instance being that of this poem, and the other the incomparable "Address to the Terrestrial Globe" in the "Bab Ballads."

There was, again, another poetic element entirely peculiar to Tennyson, which his critics have, in many cases, ridiculously confused with a fault. This was the fact that Tennyson stood alone among modern poets in the attempt to give a poetic character to the conception of Liberal Conservatism, of splendid compromise. The carping critics who have abused Tennyson for this do not see that it was far more daring and original for a poet to defend conventionality than to defend a cart-load of revolutions. His really sound and essential conception of Liberty,

"Turning to scorn with lips divine
The falsehood of extremes,"

is as good a definition of Liberalism as has been uttered in poetry in the Liberal century. Moderation is *not* a compromise; moderation is a passion; the passion of great judges. That Tennyson felt that lyrical enthusiasm could be devoted to established customs, to indefensible and ineradicable national constitutions, to the dignity of time and the empire of unutterable common sense, all this did not make him a tamer poet, but an infinitely more original one. Any poetaster can describe a thunderstorm; it requires a poet to describe the ancient and quiet sky.

I cannot, indeed, fall in with Mr. Morton Luce in his somewhat frigid and patrician theory of poetry. "Dialect," he says, "mostly falls below the dignity of art." I cannot feel myself that art has any dignity higher than the indwelling and divine dignity of human nature. Great poets like Burns were far more undignified when they clothed their thoughts in what Mr. Morton Luce calls "the seemly raiment of cultured speech" than when they clothed them in the headlong and flexible patois in which they thought and prayed and quarrelled and made love. If Tennyson failed (which I do not admit) in such poems as "The Northern Farmer," it was not because he used too much of the spirit of the dialect, but because he used too little.

Tennyson belonged undoubtedly to a period from which we are divided; the period in which men had queer ideas of the antagonism of science and religion; the period in which the Missing Link was really missing. But his hold upon the old realities of existence never wavered; he was the apostle of the sanctity of laws, of the sanctity of customs; above all, like every poet, he was the apostle of the sanctity of words.

ELIZABETH BARRETT BROWNING

The delightful new edition of Mrs. Browning's "Casa Guidi Windows" which Mr. John Lane has just issued ought certainly to serve as an opportunity for the serious criticism and inevitable admiration to which a great poet is entitled. For Mrs. Browning was a great poet, and not, as is idly and vulgarly supposed, only a great poetess. The word poetess is bad English, and it conveys a particularly bad compliment. Nothing is more remarkable about Mrs. Browning's work than the absence of that trite and namby-pamby elegance which the last two centuries demanded from lady writers. Wherever her verse is bad it is bad from some extravagance of imagery, some violence of comparison, some kind of debauch of cleverness. Her nonsense never arises from weakness, but from a confusion of powers. If the phrase explain itself, she is far more a great poet than she is a good one.

Mrs. Browning often appears more luscious and sentimental than many other literary women, but this was because she was stronger. It requires a certain amount of internal force to break down. A complete self-humiliation requires enormous strength, more strength than most of us possess. When she was writing the poetry of self-abandonment she really abandoned herself with the valour and decision of an anchorite abandoning the world. Such a couplet as:

"Our Euripides, the human,
With his dropping of warm tears,"

gives to most of us a sickly and nauseous sensation. Nothing can be well conceived more ridiculous than Euripides going about dropping tears with a loud splash, and Mrs. Browning coming after him with a thermometer. But the one emphatic point about this idiotic couplet is that Mrs. Hemans would never have written it. She would have written something perfectly dignified, perfectly harmless, perfectly inconsiderable. Mrs. Browning was in a great and serious difficulty. She really meant something. She aimed at a vivid and curious image, and she missed it. She had that catastrophic and public failure which is, as much as a medal or a testimonial, the badge of the brave.

In spite of the tiresome half truth that art is unmoral, the arts require a certain considerable number of moral qualities, and more especially all the arts require courage. The art of drawing, for example, requires even a kind of physical courage. Anyone who has tried to draw a straight line and failed knows that he fails chiefly in nerve, as he might fail to jump off a cliff. And similarly all great literary art involves the element of risk, and the greatest literary artists have commonly been those who have run the greatest risk of talking nonsense. Almost all great poets rant, from Shakespeare downwards. Mrs. Browning was Elizabethan in her luxuriance and her audacity, and the gigantic scale of her wit. We often feel with her as we feel with Shakespeare, that she would have done better with half as much talent. The great curse of the Elizabethans is upon her, that she cannot leave anything alone, she cannot write a single line without a conceit:

"And the eyes of the peacock fans
Winked at the alien glory,"

she said of the Papal fans in the presence of the Italian tricolour:

"And a royal blood sends glances up her princely eye to trouble,
And the shadow of a monarch's crown is softened in her hair,"

is her description of a beautiful and aristocratic lady. The notion of peacock feathers winking like so many London urchins is perhaps one of her rather aggressive and outrageous figures of speech. The image of a woman's hair as the softened shadow of a crown is a singularly vivid and perfect one. But both have the same quality of intellectual fancy and intellectual concentration. They are both instances of a sort of ethereal epigram. This is the great and dominant characteristic of Mrs. Browning, that she was significant alike in failure and success. Just as every marriage in the world, good or bad, is a marriage, dramatic, irrevocable, and big with coming events, so every one of her wild weddings between alien ideas is an accomplished fact which produces a certain effect on the imagination, which has for good or evil become part and parcel of our mental vision forever. She gives the reader the impression that she never declined a fancy, just as some gentlemen of the eighteenth century never declined a duel. When she fell it was always because she missed the foothold, never because she funked the leap.

"Casa Guidi Windows" is, in one aspect, a poem very typical of its author. Mrs. Browning may fairly be called the peculiar poet of Liberalism, of that great movement of the first half of the nineteenth century towards the emancipation of men from ancient institutions which had gradually changed their nature, from the houses of refuge which had turned into dungeons, and the mystic jewels which remained only as fetters. It was not what we ordinarily understand by revolt. It had no hatred in its heart for ancient and essentially human institutions. It had that deeply conservative belief in the most ancient of institutions, the average man, which goes by the name of democracy. It had none of the spirit of modern Imperialism which is kicking a man because he is down. But, on the other hand, it had none of the spirit of modern Anarchism and scepticism which is kicking a man merely because he is up. It was based fundamentally on a belief in the destiny of humanity, whether that belief took an irreligious form, as in Swinburne, or a religious form, as in Mrs. Browning. It had that rooted and natural conviction that the Millennium was coming tomorrow which has been the conviction of all iconoclasts and reformers, and for which some rationalists have been absurd enough to blame the early Christians. But they had none of that disposition to pin their whole faith to some black-and-white scientific system which afterwards became the curse of philosophical Radicalism. They were not like the sociologists who lay down a final rectification of things, amounting to nothing except an end of the world, a great deal more depressing than would be the case if it were knocked to pieces by a comet. Their ideal, like the ideal of all sensible people, was a chaotic and confused notion of goodness made up of English primroses and Greek statues, birds singing in April, and regiments being cut to pieces for a flag. They were neither Radicals nor Socialists, but Liberals, and a Liberal is a noble and indispensable lunatic who tries to make a cosmos of his own head.

Mrs. Browning and her husband were more liberal than most Liberals. Theirs was the hospitality of the intellect and the hospitality of the heart, which is the best definition of the term. They never fell into the habit of the idle revolutionists of supposing that the past was bad because the future was good, which amounted to asserting that because humanity had never made anything but mistakes it was now quite certain to be right. Browning possessed in a greater degree than any other man the power of realising that all conventions were only victorious revolutions. He could follow the mediæval logicians in all their sowing of the wind and reaping of the whirlwind with all that generous ardour which is due to abstract ideas. He could study the ancients with the young eyes of the Renaissance and read a Greek grammar like a book of love lyrics. This immense and almost confounding Liberalism of Browning doubtless had some effect upon his wife. In her vision of New Italy she went back to the image of Ancient Italy like an honest and true revolutionist; for does not the very word "revolution" mean a rolling backward. All true revolutions are reversions to the natural and the normal. A revolutionist who breaks with the past is a notion fit for an idiot. For how could a man even wish for something which he had never heard of? Mrs. Browning's inexhaustible sympathy with all the ancient and essential passions of humanity was nowhere more in evidence than in her conception of patriotism. For some dark reason, which it is difficult indeed to fathom, belief in patriotism in our day is held to mean principally a belief in every other nation abandoning its patriotic feelings. In the case of no other passion does this weird contradiction exist. Men whose lives are mainly based upon friendship sympathise with the friendships of others. The interest of engaged couples in each other is a proverb, and like many other proverbs sometimes a nuisance. In patriotism alone it is considered correct just now to assume that the sentiment does not exist in other people. It was not so with the great Liberals of Mrs. Browning's time. The Brownings had, so to speak, a disembodied talent for patriotism. They loved England and they loved Italy; yet they were the very reverse of cosmopolitans. They loved the two countries as countries, not as arbitrary divisions of the globe. They had hold of the root and essence of patriotism. They knew how certain flowers and birds and rivers pass into the mills of the brain and come out as wars and discoveries, and how some triumphant adventure or some staggering crime wrought in a remote continent may bear about it the colour of an Italian city or the soul of a silent village of Surrey.